Hands-On Python Seaborn:

A Practical Guide to Data Visualization

Sarful Hassan

Preface

Who This Book Is For
This book is for data scientists, analysts, and developers looking to master data visualization with Seaborn in Python. Whether you're a beginner or an experienced user, you'll find practical examples and techniques to enhance your skills.

How This Book Is Organized
The book is split into three sections:

1. **Getting Started**: Basics of Seaborn and plotting.

2. **Advanced Features**: Customizing plots and creating complex visualizations.

3. **Real-World Data**: Working with Seaborn for financial, environmental, and multivariate data.

What Was Left Out
This book doesn't cover advanced topics like machine learning or interactive visualizations. Focus is on Seaborn's core features and integrations.

Code Style (About the Code)
Code follows Python best practices, with clear comments and structure for easy understanding. Dependencies like Seaborn and Pandas are noted where needed.

Release Notes
This edition uses Seaborn **latest version** and Python **latest version**. Check the official documentation for updates.

Notes on the First Edition
The first edition covers the foundational features of Seaborn. Future editions will expand based on reader feedback.

MechatronicsLAB Online Learning
We offer online courses that complement this book. Visit mechatronicslab.net for more info.

How to Contact Us

For questions, reach us at:

- Email: mechatronicslab.net@gmail.com

- Website: mechatronicslab.net

Acknowledgments for the First Edition

Thanks to our families, the Seaborn development team, and the Python community for their support.

Copyright

© MechatronicsLAB, 2025. All rights reserved.

Disclaimer

The content is provided "as is" with no guarantees on accuracy. Use the information at your own risk.

Table of Contents

Chapter-1 Introduction to Python and Seaborn

Seaborn is a powerful Python library for data visualization built on top of Matplotlib. It provides a high-level interface for creating attractive and informative statistical graphics with minimal code. Seaborn integrates well with Pandas, making it ideal for visualizing datasets efficiently.

Why Python for Data Visualization?

Python is a widely used programming language in data science due to its simplicity, flexibility, and extensive ecosystem of libraries. When combined with Seaborn, Python enables users to generate elegant visualizations effortlessly.

What is Seaborn?

Seaborn is a Python visualization library designed to simplify the process of creating complex statistical plots. It enhances Matplotlib's functionality by providing built-in themes, color palettes, and functions for plotting relationships between variables.

Key Features of Seaborn

1. **Statistical Data Visualization** – Supports plots like histograms, bar charts, and violin plots for understanding data distributions.
2. **Integration with Pandas** – Works seamlessly with Pandas DataFrames, allowing quick and efficient data visualization.
3. **Built-in Themes** – Provides aesthetically pleasing color palettes and styles for publication-ready plots.
4. **Multiple Plot Types** – Supports scatter plots, line plots, box plots, pair plots, and heatmaps.
5. **Faceted Plots** – Allows visualization of data subsets using FacetGrid for multi-panel plots.
6. **Customization** – Enables easy customization of plots with labels, legends, and color schemes.

Why Use Seaborn Over Matplotlib?

1. **Simplified Syntax** – Reduces the amount of code needed to create detailed visualizations.
2. **Better Aesthetics** – Offers built-in themes for producing visually appealing graphics.

3. **Statistical Support** – Provides built-in functions for regression and categorical plots.
4. **Data Handling** – Works directly with Pandas DataFrames, eliminating the need for manual data extraction.

Applications of Seaborn

1. **Exploratory Data Analysis (EDA)** – Visualizing patterns, trends, and distributions in data.
2. **Statistical Analysis** – Creating correlation heatmaps, regression plots, and categorical comparisons.
3. **Machine Learning** – Analyzing feature relationships and model performance using visualization.
4. **Business Intelligence** – Generating reports with clear and insightful charts.

Seaborn simplifies data visualization in Python, making it an essential tool for data scientists and analysts. Its ability to create beautiful and informative plots with minimal effort makes it a preferred choice for statistical graphics.

Chapter-2 Installing and Setting Up Seaborn

Seaborn is a high-level Python visualization library built on top of Matplotlib. It simplifies the creation of complex statistical plots with minimal code. This chapter provides step-by-step instructions for installing and setting up Seaborn on different platforms, including Windows, Linux, macOS, Raspberry Pi, and Anaconda. By the end of this section, you will have Seaborn installed and ready to create data visualizations.

Step 1: Install Seaborn Using pip

The simplest way to install Seaborn is via pip, Python's package manager. Run the following command in your terminal or command prompt:

```
pip install seaborn
```

This command will install Seaborn along with its dependencies, including Matplotlib and Pandas.

Step 2: Verify the Installation

After installation, you can verify that Seaborn is correctly installed by running the following command in Python:

```
import seaborn as sns
print(sns.__version__)
```

If Seaborn is installed successfully, this command will print the installed version.

Step 3: Installing Seaborn in a Virtual Environment (Recommended)

To prevent conflicts between different packages, it is recommended to install Seaborn in a virtual environment. Follow these steps:

```
pip install virtualenv
virtualenv seaborn_env
source seaborn_env/bin/activate  # On macOS/Linux
# On Windows: seaborn_env\Scripts\activate
pip install seaborn
```

Step 4: Installing Seaborn on Different Platforms

Windows Installation

1. Ensure Python and pip are installed. Update pip if needed:
```
python -m pip install --upgrade pip
```
Install Seaborn using pip:

```
pip install seaborn
```

3. Verify the installation using Python:
```
import seaborn as sns
print(sns.__version__)
```

Linux Installation

1. Update package manager and install Python dependencies:
```
sudo apt update && sudo apt install python3-pip
python3-dev
```

2.   Install Seaborn using pip:

```
pip install seaborn
```

3.   Verify the installation using Python.

macOS Installation

1.   Install Python using Homebrew (if not already installed):

```
brew install python
```

2.   Install Seaborn via pip:

```
pip install seaborn
```

3.   Verify the installation using Python.

Raspberry Pi Installation

1.   Update system and install dependencies:

```
sudo apt update && sudo apt install python3-pip
```

2.   Install Seaborn using pip:

```
pip install seaborn
```

3.   Verify installation using Python.

Step 5: Installing Seaborn with Anaconda

If you are using Anaconda, you can install Seaborn with the following command:

```
conda install seaborn
```

This will install Seaborn and its dependencies in the Anaconda environment.
To update Seaborn in Anaconda:

```
conda update seaborn
```

Step 6: Updating Seaborn

To update Seaborn to the latest version, run:

```
pip install --upgrade seaborn
```

Step 7: Setting Up Seaborn for Use

Once Seaborn is installed, import it in Python and set up Matplotlib for inline plotting:

```
import seaborn as sns
import matplotlib.pyplot as plt
sns.set_style("darkgrid")
```

Step 8: Troubleshooting Common Issues

- **ModuleNotFoundError: No module named 'seaborn'** – Ensure that Seaborn is installed in the correct environment. Activate the environment before running Python.
- **Seaborn Plots Not Showing** – Add `plt.show()` after your plotting commands to display the plots.

Seaborn is now installed and ready to use for creating beautiful statistical visualizations.

Chapter-3 Seaborn's Integration with Matplotlib and Pandas

Seaborn is built on top of Matplotlib and integrates seamlessly with Pandas, making it a powerful tool for data visualization. This integration allows users to efficiently create complex plots while handling data in an intuitive manner. Understanding how Seaborn interacts with these libraries enables better visualization, customization, and data handling.

Seaborn and Matplotlib

Matplotlib is the fundamental visualization library in Python, and Seaborn enhances its functionality by providing high-level plotting functions, built-in statistical analysis, and aesthetic styling options.

Comparison of Matplotlib and Seaborn

Feature	Matplotlib	Seaborn
Ease of Use	Requires manual styling	Provides built-in themes and color palettes
Statistical Support	Requires additional coding	Includes built-in statistical plots
Integration with Pandas	Limited	Seamless
Default Aesthetics	Basic	Visually appealing

Key Benefits of Seaborn's Integration with Matplotlib

- Simplifies the process of creating complex statistical plots with fewer lines of code.
- Provides built-in themes and color palettes for visually appealing graphics.
- Reduces the amount of manual styling required compared to Matplotlib.
- Supports overlaying Seaborn plots on Matplotlib figures for enhanced customization.

Example: Using Seaborn with Matplotlib

```python
import seaborn as sns
import matplotlib.pyplot as plt


sns.set_style("darkgrid")  # Apply Seaborn style
data = [1, 2, 3, 4, 5, 6, 7, 8, 9]
plt.plot(data, marker='o', linestyle='-', color='b')  #
Matplotlib plot with Seaborn styling
plt.title("Example Line Plot")
plt.xlabel("X-axis")
plt.ylabel("Y-axis")
plt.show()
```

Seaborn and Pandas

Pandas is a widely used data manipulation library in Python, and Seaborn is designed to work efficiently with Pandas DataFrames. This integration allows users to visualize data directly from DataFrames without requiring manual conversions.

Comparison of Pandas and Seaborn for Data Visualization

Feature	Pandas Visualization	Seaborn
Ease of Use	Basic plotting functions	Advanced and customizable plots
Default Aesthetics	Simple	Prettier with built-in themes
Statistical Insights	Requires extra processing	Built-in statistical analysis

Key Benefits of Seaborn's Integration with Pandas

- Directly accepts Pandas DataFrames for plotting, avoiding the need for additional data transformations.
- Supports automatic detection and handling of categorical variables.
- Provides statistical functions such as correlation heatmaps, regression plots, and distribution plots.
- Enables visualization of trends, relationships, and distributions with minimal effort.

Example: Using Seaborn with Pandas

```python
import seaborn as sns
import pandas as pd
import matplotlib.pyplot as plt

# Creating a sample DataFrame
data = {"Category": ["A", "B", "C", "D"], "Values":
[10, 20, 15, 25]}
df = pd.DataFrame(data)

sns.barplot(x="Category", y="Values", data=df,
palette="viridis")
plt.title("Bar Plot of Categories")
plt.xlabel("Category")
plt.ylabel("Values")
plt.show()
```

Advanced Customization of Plots

Seaborn allows extensive customization of plots using Matplotlib functions. This helps in refining visuals for better presentation and analysis.

Example: Customizing a Box Plot

```
import seaborn as sns
import matplotlib.pyplot as plt

sns.set_style("whitegrid")
tips = sns.load_dataset("tips")

plt.figure(figsize=(10, 6))
sns.boxplot(x="day", y="total_bill", data=tips,
palette="pastel", width=0.6)
plt.title("Total Bill Distribution by Day",
fontsize=14)
plt.xlabel("Day of the Week", fontsize=12)
plt.ylabel("Total Bill ($)", fontsize=12)
plt.xticks(fontsize=10)
plt.yticks(fontsize=10)
plt.show()
```

Using Seaborn with Multiple Subplots

Seaborn can be integrated with Matplotlib's subplot functionality to display multiple visualizations in a single figure.

Example: Multiple Subplots with Seaborn

```
import seaborn as sns
import matplotlib.pyplot as plt

# Load sample dataset
tips = sns.load_dataset("tips")

# Create subplots
fig, axes = plt.subplots(1, 2, figsize=(12, 5))

sns.histplot(tips["total_bill"], kde=True, ax=axes[0],
color="blue")
```

```
axes[0].set_title("Distribution of Total Bill")

sns.scatterplot(x="total_bill", y="tip", data=tips,
hue="sex", ax=axes[1], palette="coolwarm")
axes[1].set_title("Total Bill vs Tip")

plt.tight_layout()
plt.show()
```

Conclusion

Seaborn's integration with Matplotlib and Pandas makes it an essential tool for data visualization. By leveraging these libraries together, users can efficiently analyze, customize, and present data in an intuitive and visually appealing manner. With Seaborn's built-in themes, statistical functions, and Matplotlib compatibility, users can create high-quality visualizations with minimal effort.

Chapter 4: Creating Your First Plot with Seaborn

Seaborn is a powerful Python visualization library built on top of Matplotlib. It provides an easy-to-use interface for creating informative and attractive statistical graphics. This chapter introduces Seaborn, explains its advantages over Matplotlib, and walks through the steps to create basic plots. Readers will learn to import Seaborn, load datasets, and create their first visualizations.

Key Characteristics of Seaborn:

- **Statistical Visualization:** Seaborn simplifies the creation of complex statistical plots.
- **Built-in Datasets:** Includes sample datasets for easy experimentation.
- **Integration with Pandas:** Works seamlessly with DataFrames.
- **Enhanced Aesthetics:** Provides better default styles compared to Matplotlib.
- **Efficient Plotting:** Requires less code to generate insightful visualizations.

Basic Rules for Using Seaborn:

- **Import the Seaborn library before creating plots.**
- **Load and explore the dataset to understand its structure.**
- **Choose the appropriate plot type based on the data and insights required.**
- **Customize the plot using Seaborn functions for aesthetics and clarity.**
- **Display the plot using Matplotlib's show( ) function.**

Syntax Table:

SL No	Function	Syntax Example	Description
1	Import Seaborn	`import seaborn as sns`	Imports the Seaborn library.
2	Load Dataset	`data = sns.load_dataset('tips')`	Loads a sample dataset.
3	Create a Plot	`sns.scatterplot(x='total_bill', y='tip', data=data)`	Creates a scatter plot.
4	Customiz e Style	`sns.set_style('whitegrid')`	Sets the style of the plot.
5	Show Plot	`plt.show()`	Displays the plot.

1. Import Seaborn
What is Seaborn?

Seaborn is a Python visualization library designed to make statistical graphics more intuitive and informative. It provides a high-level interface to Matplotlib, allowing users to create visually appealing plots with minimal code. Unlike Matplotlib, which requires significant styling to make plots attractive, Seaborn comes with built-in themes and color palettes that make visualizations more professional and aesthetically pleasing. Seaborn is particularly useful when dealing with complex datasets, as it supports categorical plotting, regression analysis, and multi-plot grid configurations.

Syntax:

```
import seaborn as sns
import matplotlib.pyplot as plt
```

Syntax Explanation:

- **import seaborn as sns**: This command imports the Seaborn library and assigns it the alias sns, which is commonly used in the Python community to maintain concise and readable code.
- **import matplotlib.pyplot as plt**: Since Seaborn is built on Matplotlib, this command is used to further customize and display plots. Matplotlib's show() function is often required to render Seaborn plots correctly in certain environments.

Example:

```
import seaborn as sns
import matplotlib.pyplot as plt
print("Seaborn and Matplotlib imported successfully!")
```

Example Explanation:
- This simple script confirms that Seaborn and Matplotlib are installed and can be imported without errors.
- The print statement acts as a basic check to verify that the libraries are ready for use.

2. Load a Dataset

Why Load a Dataset?
Datasets provide the foundation for data visualization. Seaborn includes several built-in datasets that allow users to experiment with various types of visualizations without needing to collect or preprocess data manually. These datasets are valuable for learning and quick prototyping before working with real-world data. The load_dataset function fetches a dataset as a Pandas DataFrame, making it easy to manipulate and analyze before plotting.

Syntax:
```
data = sns.load_dataset('tips')
print(data.head())
```

Syntax Explanation:
- **sns.load_dataset('tips')**: Loads the built-in tips dataset, which contains information about restaurant bills, tips, and customer demographics. This dataset is commonly used to demonstrate various Seaborn plotting techniques.
- **print(data.head())**: Displays the first five rows of the dataset, providing insight into its structure and contents. This helps in understanding the available columns and their data types.

Example:
```
print("Dataset Overview:")
print(data.info())
print(data.describe())
```

Example Explanation:
- **data.info()**: Displays the dataset's column names, data types, and missing values, which helps in assessing data quality.
- **data.describe()**: Provides summary statistics such as mean, median, standard deviation, and percentile values for numerical columns.
- These functions are useful for gaining a preliminary understanding of the dataset before proceeding with visualization.

3. Create Your First Plot

What is a Scatter Plot?
A scatter plot is a type of data visualization that represents individual data points on a two-dimensional plane. Each point's position is determined by two numerical variables—one plotted on the x-axis and the other on the y-axis. Scatter plots are particularly useful for identifying correlations, trends, and patterns in the data, as well as detecting outliers that deviate significantly from the general distribution.

Syntax:
```
sns.scatterplot(x='total_bill', y='tip', data=data)
plt.show()
```
Syntax Explanation:
- **sns.scatterplot(x='total_bill', y='tip', data=data)**: Generates a scatter plot where the x-axis represents total bill amounts and the y-axis represents tip amounts.
- **plt.show()**: Ensures that the plot is displayed correctly in environments where explicit rendering is required.

Example:
```
sns.scatterplot(x='total_bill', y='tip', hue='sex', data=data)
plt.show()
```
Example Explanation:
- **hue='sex'**: Differentiates data points by gender, allowing for comparison of tipping behavior between male and female customers.

- This additional attribute enhances the interpretability of the scatter plot by introducing categorical color coding.

4. Customize Style

What is Customizing Style?

Customizing the style of a plot allows users to enhance readability and aesthetics. Seaborn provides several built-in themes such as `darkgrid`, `whitegrid`, `dark`, `white`, and `ticks`, which help improve visual clarity. Adjusting the style can make data patterns easier to interpret and enhance presentation quality.

Syntax:

```
sns.set_style('whitegrid')
sns.scatterplot(x='total_bill', y='tip', data=data)
plt.show()
```

Syntax Explanation:
- **`sns.set_style('whitegrid')`**: Applies a clean white grid background to the plot, improving visibility of data points.
- **The scatter plot is recreated with the improved style.**

Example:

```
sns.set_style('darkgrid')
sns.scatterplot(x='total_bill', y='tip', data=data)
plt.show()
```

Example Explanation:
- **The darkgrid style provides a dark background with visible grid lines,** making data points stand out.
- Helps differentiate between categories while maintaining a professional appearance.

5. Show Plot

What is Showing a Plot?

Displaying a plot is the final step in visualization. Matplotlib's `show()` function ensures that the plot is rendered correctly in all environments, including Jupyter Notebooks and standalone Python scripts.

Syntax:

```
plt.show()
```

Syntax Explanation:

- **plt.show()**: Renders the plot and makes it visible to the user.
- Ensures compatibility across different programming environments.

Example:
```
sns.scatterplot(x='total_bill', y='tip', data=data)
plt.show()
```
Example Explanation:

- Displays a scatter plot showing the relationship between total_bill and tip.
- Ensures the visualization is correctly presented before saving or exporting it.

6. Real-World Project: Analyzing Restaurant Tips

This project involves analyzing tipping behavior in a restaurant using Seaborn. We will visualize relationships between total bill amounts, tip sizes, and other categorical features such as gender and time of dining. By the end of this project, we will gain insights into tipping trends and customer behavior.

Steps to Follow:

1. **Load and Explore the Dataset**
   a. Load the built-in tips dataset using Seaborn.
   b. Explore its structure and statistical summary.
2. **Create Visualizations**
   a. Generate scatter plots to examine correlations between total_bill and tip.
   b. Use categorical color coding (hue) to distinguish tipping behavior by gender.
   c. Experiment with different Seaborn styles to enhance clarity.
3. **Analyze and Interpret Trends**
   a. Identify patterns in tipping amounts based on meal time (lunch vs. dinner).
   b. Compare tipping behavior between male and female customers.

      c.   Investigate the influence of table size on tip percentages.

4. Save and Present Findings

      a.   Save the final plots for report generation.

      b.   Summarize insights in a data visualization report.

Example Code:

```
import seaborn as sns
import matplotlib.pyplot as plt


# Load dataset
data = sns.load_dataset('tips')


# Set style
sns.set_style('whitegrid')


# Create scatter plot with hue for gender
differentiation
sns.scatterplot(x='total_bill', y='tip', hue='sex',
data=data)


# Show and save plot
plt.savefig('tips_analysis.png')
plt.show()
```

Expected Result:

The scatter plot should clearly visualize the relationship between total_bill and tip, with different colors representing different genders. Users should be able to identify trends, such as whether higher total bills correlate with higher tips and whether tipping behavior differs based on gender. Additionally, the plot should be aesthetically enhanced by the Seaborn whitegrid style.

- **Clear trend observation:** Users should see whether tips increase with the total bill amount.
- **Gender differentiation:** The use of hue='sex' ensures that male and female customers' tipping behaviors are visually distinguishable.
- **Improved readability:** The whitegrid style enhances the overall

clarity of the visualization.
- **Saved visualization:** The plot should be saved as `tips_analysis.png` for future reference or reporting.

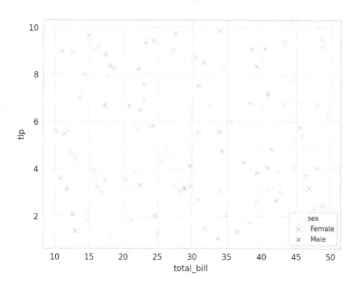

Example Explanation:

- `sns.scatterplot(x='total_bill', y='tip', hue='sex', data=data)`: Creates a scatter plot with gender differentiation.
- `sns.set_style('whitegrid')`: Improves the clarity of the plot.
- `plt.savefig('tips_analysis.png')`: Saves the visualization for future reference.
- `plt.show()`: Displays the final plot for analysis.

This project helps in understanding how visualization can reveal insights from real-world datasets, making data-driven decision-making more effective.

Chapter 5: Scatter Plots and Line Plots with Seaborn

In this chapter, we explore scatter plots and line plots using Seaborn. Scatter plots are used to display the relationship between two numerical variables, while line plots help visualize trends over time or ordered sequences. Seaborn provides an intuitive and efficient way to create these plots with minimal coding effort. This chapter covers syntax, customization, and real-world applications of scatter and line plots.

Key Characteristics of Scatter and Line Plots:

- **Scatter Plots:**
    - Display individual data points based on two numerical variables.
    - Help identify correlations, clusters, and outliers.
    - Can be customized using colors, markers, and sizes.
- **Line Plots:**
    - Show trends over time or ordered data.
    - Useful for time series and sequential data visualization.
    - Support multiple line plotting with different styles.

Basic Rules for Creating Scatter and Line Plots:

- **Load and prepare the dataset** before plotting.
- **Choose the appropriate plot type** based on the data and insights required.
- **Customize the visualization** using Seaborn's built-in features like hue, style, and size.
- **Use informative labels and titles** to improve readability.
- **Save and share the final plots** for reporting and presentation.

Syntax Table:

SL No	Function	Syntax Example	Description
1	Import Seaborn	`import seaborn as sns`	Imports the Seaborn library.
2	Load Dataset	`data = sns.load_dataset('tips')`	Loads a dataset for visualization.

3	Create Scatter Plot	`sns.scatterplot(x='total _bill', y='tip', data=data)`	Generates a scatter plot.
4	Create Line Plot	`sns.lineplot(x='day', y='total_bill', data=data)`	Generates a line plot.
5	Show Plot	`plt.show()`	Displays the created plot.

1. Scatter Plots

What is a Scatter Plot?

A scatter plot represents individual data points on a two-dimensional plane, with each point determined by two numerical variables. This type of visualization is widely used for identifying relationships, detecting outliers, and clustering observations. Scatter plots can be particularly useful in statistical analysis and machine learning for understanding the distribution of data and the potential correlation between two features. With Seaborn, scatter plots can be easily created and customized using additional attributes like hue, style, and size.

Syntax:

```
import seaborn as sns
import matplotlib.pyplot as plt

data = sns.load_dataset('tips')
sns.scatterplot(x='total_bill', y='tip', hue='sex',
data=data)
plt.show()
```

Syntax Explanation:

- **`sns.scatterplot(x='total_bill', y='tip', hue='sex', data=data)`**: This command generates a scatter plot where the `total_bill` values are plotted on the x-axis and `tip` values on the y-axis. The `hue='sex'` parameter adds color differentiation to categorize data points based on gender.
- **`plt.show()`**: Displays the generated plot and ensures it appears correctly.

Example:

```
sns.scatterplot(x='total_bill', y='tip', hue='time',
style='sex', data=data)
plt.show()
```

Example Explanation:

- Uses **hue='time'** to categorize points based on meal time (Lunch or Dinner), allowing users to see tipping behavior variations.
- Uses **style='sex'** to differentiate gender through different marker styles.
- This visualization provides a deeper understanding of customer tipping patterns.

2. Line Plots

What is a Line Plot?

A line plot is used to represent trends over time or ordered data points, with each point connected by a continuous line. These plots are widely used in financial analysis, stock market trends, and scientific research to observe data fluctuations over a specific period. Seaborn's lineplot function provides an easy way to generate such visualizations, incorporating multiple lines for different categories and allowing for extensive customization.

Syntax:

```
sns.lineplot(x='day', y='total_bill', data=data)
plt.show()
```

Syntax Explanation:

- **sns.lineplot(x='day', y='total_bill', data=data):** Creates a line plot where day represents the x-axis and total_bill represents the y-axis, helping to visualize the variation of restaurant earnings over the days of the week.
- **plt.show():** Ensures the plot is displayed correctly.

Example:
```
sns.lineplot(x='day', y='total_bill', hue='sex',
style='sex', data=data)
plt.show()
```

Example Explanation:
- **hue='sex'**: Differentiates line colors based on gender, making it easier to compare trends.
- **style='sex'**: Varies the line style for different genders, improving visual interpretation.
- This allows for trend analysis of spending patterns between male and female customers over a week.

3. Create a Scatter Plot

What is a Scatter Plot?
A scatter plot is a graphical representation where individual data points are plotted along two numerical axes. It is particularly useful for identifying relationships, trends, and potential correlations between two variables.
Syntax:
```
sns.scatterplot(x='total_bill', y='tip', hue='sex',
style='time', data=data)
plt.show()
```

Syntax Explanation:
- **sns.scatterplot(x='total_bill', y='tip', hue='sex', style='time', data=data)**: Generates a scatter plot where the x-axis represents total bill amounts and the y-axis represents tip amounts. The hue parameter differentiates gender by color, and the style parameter changes marker types based on meal time.
- **plt.show()**: Ensures the plot is displayed correctly.

Example:
```
sns.scatterplot(x='total_bill', y='tip', hue='day',
style='sex', size='size', data=data)
plt.show()
```

Example Explanation:
- **hue='day'**: Colors points based on the day of the week.
- **style='sex'**: Differentiates genders by marker style.
- **size='size'**: Adjusts the marker size according to party size.
- This visualization helps analyze tipping behavior across different days and meal groups.

4. Create a Line Plot

What is a Line Plot?
A line plot is used to show trends or patterns in data over time or ordered sequences. It is commonly used in time-series analysis, financial trends, and scientific research.

Syntax:
```
sns.lineplot(x='day', y='total_bill', hue='sex',
style='sex', markers=True, data=data)
plt.show()
```

Syntax Explanation:
- **sns.lineplot(x='day', y='total_bill', hue='sex', style='sex', markers=True, data=data)**: Generates a line plot showing how total bill amounts change over the days of the week, with gender differentiation.
- **plt.show()**: Ensures the plot is displayed properly.

Example:
```
sns.lineplot(x='size', y='total_bill', hue='time',
style='sex', markers=True, data=data)
plt.show()
```

Example Explanation:
- **hue='time'**: Differentiates meal times (Lunch/Dinner) using colors.
- **style='sex'**: Uses different line styles for gender differentiation.
- **markers=True**: Adds markers to improve readability.
- Helps identify spending trends based on party size and meal time.

5. Show Plot

What is Showing a Plot?
Displaying a plot is the final step in visualization. Using `plt.show()` ensures that the plot is rendered correctly in all environments.
Syntax:
`plt.show()`

Syntax Explanation:
- **`plt.show()`**: Renders the plot and ensures it is visible in all output environments, including Jupyter Notebook and Python scripts.

Example:
```
sns.scatterplot(x='total_bill', y='tip', data=data)
plt.show()
```

Example Explanation:
- Displays a scatter plot visualizing the relationship between `total_bill` and `tip`.
- Ensures that all elements of the plot, such as labels and legends, are properly displayed.

Real-World Project: Analyzing Restaurant Sales Data

This project involves analyzing restaurant sales and tipping behavior using scatter and line plots. By visualizing the relationship between total bill amounts, tip sizes, and dining patterns, we aim to uncover insights into customer behavior and spending trends.
Steps:
1. **Load and Explore the Dataset**
   a. Load the `tips` dataset using Seaborn.
   b. Check dataset structure and summary statistics.
2. **Create a Scatter Plot**
   a. Visualize the relationship between `total_bill` and `tip`.
   b. Differentiate by categorical features like gender and time of dining.
3. **Create a Line Plot**

a. Examine how `total_bill` trends over different days of the week.

b. Compare spending habits between male and female customers.

4. **Customize the Plots**

    a. Adjust color schemes and styles to enhance readability.

    b. Use markers and legends to distinguish categories clearly.

5. **Save and Present the Findings**

    a. Save the final plots for reporting.

    b. Summarize insights into tipping behavior and customer trends.

Example Code:

```python
import seaborn as sns
import matplotlib.pyplot as plt

data = sns.load_dataset('tips')

# Set plot style
sns.set_style('whitegrid')

# Scatter plot
sns.scatterplot(x='total_bill', y='tip', hue='sex',
style='time', data=data)
plt.show()

# Line plot
sns.lineplot(x='day', y='total_bill', hue='sex',
style='sex', data=data)
plt.show()
```

Expected Result:

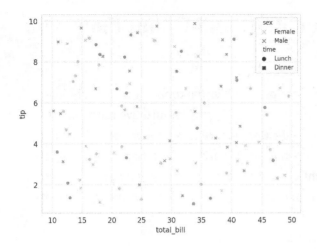

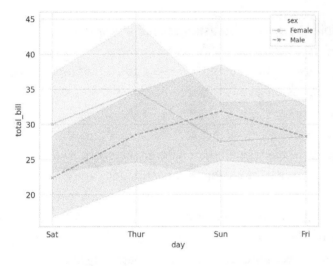

Example Explanation:

- **Scatter Plot:** Helps identify relationships between bill amounts and tipping behavior, with gender and dining time differentiation.
- **Line Plot:** Shows variations in total bill amounts over different days of the week.
- **Customization:** Improves clarity and aesthetic appeal.
- **Saved Plots:** Can be used for further analysis and reporting.

This project demonstrates how visualization techniques can uncover patterns and insights in business and customer behavior.

Chapter 6: Bar Plots and Count Plots with Seaborn

Bar plots and count plots are powerful visual tools used for analyzing categorical data distributions. Seaborn provides intuitive functions to create these plots effortlessly. Bar plots represent summary statistics (such as mean or sum) of a numerical variable for different categorical variables, whereas count plots show the frequency of different categories. This chapter covers how to create, customize, and interpret these plots using Seaborn.

Key Characteristics of Bar and Count Plots:
- **Bar Plots:**
  - Display aggregated statistics of a numerical variable across categorical groups.
  - Often used for comparing averages, totals, or proportions.
  - Can be customized with different color palettes and orientations.
- **Count Plots:**
  - Represent the frequency of different categorical values.
  - Useful for understanding data distributions at a glance.
  - Can be grouped using hue to compare multiple categories.

Basic Rules for Creating Bar and Count Plots:
- **Load and prepare the dataset** before plotting.
- **Choose between bar plots and count plots** based on whether numerical aggregation is needed.
- **Use hue and dodge parameters** to compare multiple categories in one plot.
- **Customize the visualization** with colors, labels, and styles.
- **Ensure clarity** by adding informative titles and legends.

Syntax Table:

SL No	Function	Syntax Example	Description
1	Import Seaborn	`import seaborn as sns`	Imports the Seaborn library.

2	Load Dataset	`data = sns.load_dataset('titanic')`	Loads a dataset for visualization.
3	Create Bar Plot	`sns.barplot(x='class', y='fare', data=data)`	Generates a bar plot.
4	Create Count Plot	`sns.countplot(x='sex', data=data)`	Generates a count plot.
5	Show Plot	`plt.show()`	Displays the created plot.

1. Bar Plots

What is a Bar Plot?

A bar plot represents a categorical variable on the x-axis and an aggregated numerical value (such as mean, sum, or median) on the y-axis. This type of plot is useful for comparing different groups.

Syntax:

```
import seaborn as sns
import matplotlib.pyplot as plt
data = sns.load_dataset('titanic')
sns.barplot(x='class', y='fare', data=data)
plt.show()
```

Syntax Explanation:

- **`sns.barplot(x='class', y='fare', data=data)`:** Creates a bar plot where the x-axis represents the passenger class, and the y-axis represents the average fare paid.
- **`plt.show()`:** Displays the generated plot.

Example:

```
sns.barplot(x='sex', y='survived', hue='class', data=data)
plt.show()
```

Example Explanation:

- **`hue='class'`:** Differentiates survival rates by passenger class.
- **Useful for understanding how gender and class influenced survival rates.**

2. Count Plots

What is a Count Plot?
A count plot is a specialized bar plot used to display the frequency of categorical values. Unlike a bar plot, it does not require a numerical variable for aggregation.

Syntax:
```
sns.countplot(x='sex', data=data)
plt.show()
```

Syntax Explanation:
- **sns.countplot(x='sex', data=data)**: Creates a count plot showing the number of male and female passengers in the dataset.
- **plt.show()**: Ensures the plot is rendered correctly.

Example:
```
sns.countplot(x='embark_town', hue='sex', data=data)
plt.show()
```

Example Explanation:
- **hue='sex'**: Colors bars based on gender.
- **Allows comparison of embarkation counts for male and female passengers.**

3. Customizing Bar and Count Plots

What is Customizing Bar and Count Plots?
Customization in Seaborn allows users to enhance the visual appeal and readability of bar and count plots. Modifying colors, labels, styles, and other attributes ensures that the data is presented clearly and effectively. Seaborn provides multiple options for adjusting these aesthetics.

Syntax:
```
sns.set_style('whitegrid')
sns.barplot(x='class', y='fare', hue='sex', data=data,
palette='coolwarm')
plt.show()
```

Syntax Explanation:
- **sns.set_style('whitegrid')**: Sets the background style of the plot to white grid.

- **`sns.barplot(x='class', y='fare', hue='sex', data=data, palette='coolwarm')`**: Generates a bar plot with different colors assigned to each gender using the `coolwarm` palette.
- **`plt.show()`**: Ensures that the plot is displayed correctly.

Example:
```
sns.set_style('darkgrid')
sns.countplot(x='who', hue='survived', data=data,
palette='muted')
plt.show()
```

Example Explanation:
- **`palette='muted'`**: Uses a subtle color theme for better contrast.
- **`hue='survived'`**: Differentiates survivors and non-survivors with different colors.
- **This customization enhances visual clarity and makes it easier to compare survival rates across different groups.**

4. Create Count Plot

What is a Count Plot?
A count plot is a type of bar plot that represents the frequency of categorical data. It does not require numerical aggregation, making it ideal for understanding the distribution of different categories in a dataset.

Syntax:
```
sns.countplot(x='sex', data=data)
plt.show()
```

Syntax Explanation:
- **`sns.countplot(x='sex', data=data)`**: Creates a count plot where the x-axis represents different categories (`sex` in this case) and the y-axis represents the count of occurrences in the dataset.
- **`plt.show()`**: Ensures the plot is rendered and displayed correctly.

Example:

```
sns.countplot(x='embark_town', hue='sex', data=data)
plt.show()
```

Example Explanation:

- **hue='sex'**: Differentiates counts by gender, displaying male and female data in separate colors.
- **This visualization helps analyze the distribution of embarkation points across genders, providing insights into demographic trends in the dataset.**

Real-World Project: Analyzing Titanic Passenger Data

This project uses bar and count plots to analyze passenger demographics and survival trends from the Titanic dataset.

Steps:

1. **Load and explore the dataset.**
2. **Create a count plot** to visualize gender distribution.
3. **Create a bar plot** to compare survival rates across different classes.
4. **Customize the plots** to enhance readability.
5. **Save and present the findings.**

Example Code:

```
import seaborn as sns
import matplotlib.pyplot as plt
data = sns.load_dataset('titanic')
# Set style
sns.set_style('whitegrid')
# Count plot
sns.countplot(x='sex', data=data)
plt.show()
# Bar plot
sns.barplot(x='class', y='survived', hue='sex',
data=data)
plt.show()
```

Expected Result:

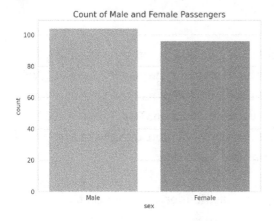

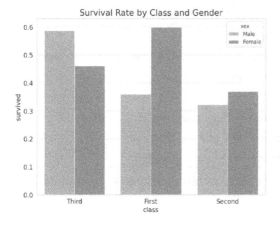

- **Count Plot:** Visualizes the distribution of male and female passengers.
- **Bar Plot:** Shows survival rates across different classes and genders.
- **Customization:** Enhances clarity and presentation.
- **Saved Plots:** Can be used for analysis and reporting.

Conclusion:

This chapter covered bar and count plots in Seaborn, including their syntax, customization, and real-world applications. By mastering these plots, you can effectively analyze categorical data distributions and trends.

Chapter 7: Histograms and KDE Plots with Seaborn

Histograms and Kernel Density Estimation (KDE) plots are essential tools for understanding data distribution. Histograms display the frequency of data points within specific intervals, while KDE plots provide a smoothed estimate of the data's probability density function. This chapter covers how to create, customize, and interpret these plots using Seaborn.

Key Characteristics of Histograms and KDE Plots:

- **Histograms:**
    - Show the frequency distribution of numerical data.
    - Useful for identifying skewness, outliers, and modality.
    - Can be customized with different bin sizes and styles.
- **KDE Plots:**
    - Provide a smooth estimate of the distribution's shape.
    - Useful for comparing distributions without discrete binning.
    - Can be combined with histograms for better visualization.

Basic Rules for Creating Histograms and KDE Plots:

- **Load and prepare the dataset** before plotting.
- **Choose appropriate bin sizes** for histograms to avoid misleading interpretations.
- **Use KDE plots for smooth distribution visualization** without abrupt bin edges.
- **Combine both plots** when necessary to enhance insights.
- **Customize the visualization** with colors, labels, and transparency settings.

Syntax Table:

SL No	Function	Syntax Example	Description
1	Import Seaborn	`import seaborn as sns`	Imports the Seaborn library.
2	Load Dataset	`data = sns.load_dataset('penguins')`	Loads a dataset for visualization.

3	Create Histogram	`sns.histplot(data['bill_length_mm'])`	Generates a histogram.
4	Create KDE Plot	`sns.kdeplot(data['bill_length_mm'])`	Generates a KDE plot.
5	Show Plot	`plt.show()`	Displays the created plot.

1. Histograms

What is a Histogram?

A histogram represents the distribution of numerical data by dividing values into bins and counting how many values fall into each bin. This visualization helps identify patterns such as skewness, modality, and outliers.

Syntax:

```
import seaborn as sns
import matplotlib.pyplot as plt

data = sns.load_dataset('penguins')
sns.histplot(data['bill_length_mm'], bins=20, kde=True)
plt.show()
```

Syntax Explanation:

- **sns.histplot(data['bill_length_mm'], bins=20, kde=True)**: Creates a histogram with 20 bins and overlays a KDE plot.
- **plt.show()**: Ensures the generated plot is displayed.

Example:

```
sns.histplot(data=data, x='bill_length_mm',
hue='species', bins=15, element='step', kde=True)
plt.show()
```

Example Explanation:

- **hue='species'**: Differentiates distributions by species.
- **element='step'**: Displays a stepped histogram for better clarity.
- **Combining KDE helps in understanding density distributions more intuitively.**

2. KDE Plots

What is a KDE Plot?

A Kernel Density Estimation (KDE) plot is a smoothed representation of a dataset's probability density. It helps in understanding the overall shape of a distribution without being affected by binning choices.

Syntax:

```
sns.kdeplot(data['bill_length_mm'], shade=True)
plt.show()
```

Syntax Explanation:

- **sns.kdeplot(data['bill_length_mm'], shade=True)**: Generates a KDE plot with shading to highlight the density.
- **plt.show()**: Ensures the plot is properly rendered.

Example:

```
sns.kdeplot(data=data, x='bill_length_mm',
hue='species', fill=True)
plt.show()
```

Example Explanation:

- **hue='species'**: Differentiates distributions by species.
- **fill=True**: Fills the KDE plot for better readability.
- **Useful for comparing multiple distributions simultaneously.**

3. Customizing Histograms and KDE Plots

What is Customizing Histograms and KDE Plots?

Customization enhances the readability and presentation of histograms and KDE plots, allowing better insights into the data distribution. Seaborn provides numerous styling options, such as adjusting colors, bin sizes, line styles, and transparency to improve visualization clarity.

Syntax:

```
sns.set_style('whitegrid')
sns.histplot(data=data, x='bill_length_mm', bins=30,
color='blue', alpha=0.6)
plt.show()
```

Syntax Explanation:

- **sns.set_style('whitegrid')**: Sets the background style of the plot to a white grid for better readability.
- **sns.histplot(data=data, x='bill_length_mm', bins=30, color='blue', alpha=0.6)**: Creates a histogram with 30 bins, applying a blue color with 60% transparency.
- **plt.show()**: Ensures the plot is displayed correctly.

Example:

```
sns.kdeplot(data=data, x='bill_length_mm', color='red',
linewidth=2, linestyle='dashed')
plt.show()
```

Example Explanation:

- **color='red'**: Sets the KDE line color to red for better contrast.
- **linewidth=2**: Increases the thickness of the KDE curve to improve visibility.
- **linestyle='dashed'**: Uses a dashed line style to differentiate KDE plots from histograms.

4. Create KDE Plot

What is a KDE Plot?
A Kernel Density Estimation (KDE) plot is a smoothed representation of a dataset's probability density. It helps in understanding the overall shape of a distribution without being affected by binning choices, unlike histograms.

Syntax:

```
sns.kdeplot(data['bill_length_mm'], shade=True)
plt.show()
```

Syntax Explanation:

- **sns.kdeplot(data['bill_length_mm'], shade=True)**: Generates a KDE plot with shading to highlight the density of values.
- **plt.show()**: Ensures the KDE plot is properly displayed.

Example:

```
sns.kdeplot(data=data, x='bill_length_mm',
hue='species', fill=True)
plt.show()
```

Example Explanation:
- **hue='species'**: Differentiates distributions by species, providing comparative insights.
- **fill=True**: Fills the KDE plot for better readability and improved visualization.
- **Useful for comparing multiple distributions simultaneously, allowing easy differentiation between categories.**

Real-World Project: Analyzing Penguin Bill Lengths

This project analyzes the distribution of penguin bill lengths using histograms and KDE plots.

Steps:
1. **Load and explore the dataset.**
2. **Create a histogram** to visualize the distribution of bill lengths.
3. **Create a KDE plot** to compare distributions by species.
4. **Customize the plots** to improve clarity.
5. **Save and present the findings.**

Example Code:

```
import seaborn as sns
import matplotlib.pyplot as plt
data = sns.load_dataset('penguins')
# Set style
sns.set_style('whitegrid')
# Histogram
sns.histplot(data=data, x='bill_length_mm',
hue='species', bins=20, kde=True)
plt.show()
# KDE Plot
sns.kdeplot(data=data, x='bill_length_mm',
hue='species', fill=True)
plt.show()
```

Expected Result:

Histogram with KDE Overlay

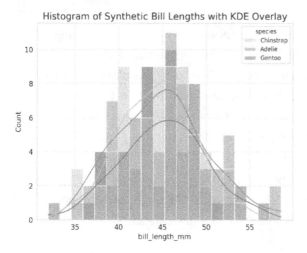

Histogram of Synthetic Bill Lengths with KDE Overlay

KDE Plot

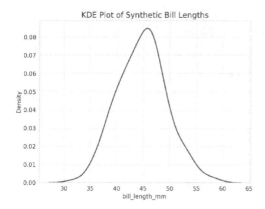

KDE Plot of Synthetic Bill Lengths

- **Histogram:** Displays the frequency distribution of bill lengths.
- **KDE Plot:** Provides a smooth density estimate for each species.
- **Customization:** Enhances clarity and insight.
- **Saved Plots:** Can be used for further statistical analysis.

Conclusion:

This chapter covered histograms and KDE plots in Seaborn, including their syntax, customization, and real-world applications. By mastering these plots, you can effectively analyze data distributions and gain deeper insights into numerical data trends.

Chapter 8: Box Plots and Violin Plots with Seaborn

Box plots and violin plots are powerful visual tools for summarizing numerical data distributions. Box plots help in identifying medians, quartiles, and outliers, while violin plots combine box plot features with a density estimation to show the full data distribution. This chapter explores how to create, customize, and interpret these plots using Seaborn.

Key Characteristics of Box Plots and Violin Plots:

- **Box Plots:**
    - Represent data distribution through quartiles.
    - Highlight median, interquartile range, and outliers.
    - Useful for comparing multiple categories.
- **Violin Plots:**
    - Extend box plots with a KDE for better visualization.
    - Show data density while preserving statistical summary.
    - Useful for analyzing multi-modal distributions.

Basic Rules for Creating Box and Violin Plots:

- **Load and preprocess the dataset** before visualization.
- **Use box plots for statistical summaries** and outlier detection.
- **Use violin plots when a density-based approach** provides more insight.
- **Customize the visualization** with hue, split, and color adjustments.
- **Combine both plots** when necessary to enhance insights.

Syntax Table:

SL No	Function	Syntax Example	Description
1	Import Seaborn	`import seaborn as sns`	Imports the Seaborn library.
2	Load Dataset	`data = sns.load_dataset('tips')`	Loads a dataset for visualization.
3	Create Box Plot	`sns.boxplot(x='day', y='total_bill', data=data)`	Generates a box plot.

4	Create Violin Plot	`sns.violinplot(x='day', y='total_bill', data=data)`	Generates a violin plot.
5	Show Plot	`plt.show()`	Displays the created plot.

1. Box Plots

What is a Box Plot?

A box plot, also known as a whisker plot, visualizes the distribution of numerical data through quartiles. It highlights the median, interquartile range (IQR), and potential outliers, making it useful for comparing distributions across categories.

Syntax:

```
import seaborn as sns
import matplotlib.pyplot as plt

data = sns.load_dataset('tips')
sns.boxplot(x='day', y='total_bill', hue='sex',
data=data)
plt.show()
```

Syntax Explanation:

- **sns.boxplot(x='day', y='total_bill', hue='sex', data=data)**: Creates a box plot where total_bill is plotted across different days, with color differentiation for gender.
- **plt.show()**: Ensures the generated plot is displayed.

Example:

```
sns.boxplot(x='sex', y='tip', hue='time', data=data)
plt.show()
```

Example Explanation:

- **hue='time'**: Differentiates distributions based on meal time (Lunch/Dinner).
- **Useful for analyzing tipping behavior variations across genders and meal times.**

2. Violin Plots

What is a Violin Plot?

A violin plot is a hybrid of a box plot and a KDE plot, providing both statistical summaries and a smoothed density estimate. It is particularly useful for analyzing the shape of distributions while retaining key summary statistics.

Syntax:

```
sns.violinplot(x='day', y='total_bill', data=data)
plt.show()
```

Syntax Explanation:

- **sns.violinplot(x='day', y='total_bill', data=data)**: Generates a violin plot displaying the density and quartiles of total bill amounts across different days.
- **plt.show()**: Ensures the plot is properly rendered.

Example:

```
sns.violinplot(x='sex', y='tip', hue='smoker',
data=data, split=True)
plt.show()
```

Example Explanation:

- **hue='smoker'**: Differentiates smokers and non-smokers within each gender.
- **split=True**: Splits the violin into two halves for easier comparison.
- **Useful for assessing how smoking habits impact tipping behavior.**

3. Customizing Box and Violin Plots

What is Customizing Box and Violin Plots?

Customization allows for improved readability and better insights by adjusting plot aesthetics such as color, width, and style. Seaborn provides options to modify the visual aspects of box and violin plots to enhance clarity and impact.

Syntax:
```
sns.set_style('whitegrid')
sns.boxplot(x='day', y='total_bill', data=data,
palette='coolwarm')
plt.show()
```

Syntax Explanation:
- **sns.set_style('whitegrid')**: Applies a white grid background for better contrast.
- **sns.boxplot(x='day', y='total_bill', data=data, palette='coolwarm')**: Creates a box plot with a color palette that enhances visibility.
- **plt.show()**: Ensures the plot is displayed properly.

Example:
```
sns.violinplot(x='day', y='total_bill', data=data,
palette='muted', inner='quartile')
plt.show()
```

Example Explanation:
- **palette='muted'**: Uses a subtle color theme for a softer visual appearance.
- **inner='quartile'**: Displays the quartile lines inside the violin plot to add statistical insight.
- **Enhances interpretability by combining summary statistics with density estimation.**

4. Create Violin Plot

What is a Violin Plot?
A violin plot is a combination of a box plot and a KDE plot. It shows the distribution of numerical data by displaying density estimation while also providing quartiles and outliers. Violin plots are particularly useful when comparing distributions across different categories while maintaining the full shape of the data.

Syntax:
```
sns.violinplot(x='day', y='total_bill', data=data)
plt.show()
```

Syntax Explanation:

- `sns.violinplot(x='day', y='total_bill', data=data)`: Creates a violin plot where the x-axis represents the day and the y-axis represents total bill amounts.
- `plt.show()`: Ensures the plot is displayed correctly.

Example:
```
sns.violinplot(x='sex', y='tip', hue='smoker',
data=data, split=True)
plt.show()
```

Example Explanation:

- `hue='smoker'`: Differentiates smokers and non-smokers within each gender.
- `split=True`: Splits the violin into two halves to provide a direct comparison.
- **This visualization helps in understanding the impact of smoking habits on tipping behavior.****

Real-World Project: Analyzing Restaurant Spending Trends

This project analyzes restaurant spending trends using box plots and violin plots.

Steps:

1. **Load and explore the dataset.**
2. **Create a box plot** to compare total bills across different days.
3. **Create a violin plot** to visualize spending trends with density estimation.
4. **Customize the plots** to improve clarity.
5. **Save and present the findings.**

Example Code:
```
import seaborn as sns
import matplotlib.pyplot as plt

data = sns.load_dataset('tips')

# Set style
```

```
sns.set_style('whitegrid')

# Box Plot
sns.boxplot(x='day', y='total_bill', hue='sex',
data=data)
plt.show()

# Violin Plot
sns.violinplot(x='day', y='total_bill', hue='sex',
data=data, split=True)
plt.show()
```

Expected Result:

Box Plot

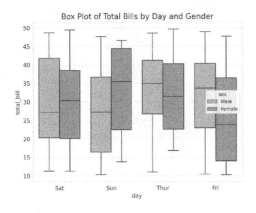

Violin Plot

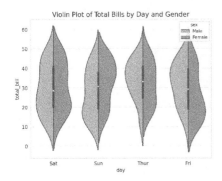

- **Box Plot:** Displays the statistical distribution of total bills across different days.
- **Violin Plot:** Provides a smooth density estimate while preserving key summary statistics.
- **Customization:** Enhances readability and insight.
- **Saved Plots:** Can be used for further business analysis.

Conclusion:

This chapter covered box plots and violin plots in Seaborn, including their syntax, customization, and real-world applications. By mastering these plots, you can effectively analyze data distributions and gain deeper insights into categorical trends.

Chapter 9: Swarm Plots and Strip Plots with Seaborn

Swarm plots and strip plots are effective visualization techniques for displaying the distribution of categorical data points. While strip plots simply plot all points along a category axis, swarm plots use an intelligent algorithm to avoid overlapping points, making them more readable. This chapter explores how to create, customize, and interpret these plots using Seaborn.

Key Characteristics of Swarm Plots and Strip Plots:

- **Swarm Plots:**
    - Position data points to avoid overlap while maintaining category alignment.
    - Useful for visualizing individual observations within categories.
    - Ideal for datasets with small to medium sample sizes.
- **Strip Plots:**
    - Display all data points along a categorical axis.
    - Allow overlapping of points unless jitter is applied.
    - Work well for comparing distributions without density estimation.

Basic Rules for Creating Swarm and Strip Plots:

- **Load and preprocess the dataset** before visualization.
- **Use swarm plots to prevent overlapping** and improve readability.
- **Use strip plots for simple scatter-like visualization** along a categorical axis.
- **Apply jitter to strip plots** to reduce point overlap and increase clarity.
- **Customize plots** using hue, palette, and size adjustments.

Syntax Table:

SL No	Function	Syntax Example	Description
1	Import Seaborn	`import seaborn as sns`	Imports the Seaborn library.
2	Load Dataset	`data = sns.load_dataset('tips')`	Loads a dataset for visualization.
3	Create Swarm Plot	`sns.swarmplot(x='day', y='total_bill', data=data)`	Generates a swarm plot.
4	Create Strip Plot	`sns.stripplot(x='day', y='total_bill', data=data)`	Generates a strip plot.
5	Show Plot	`plt.show()`	Displays the created plot.

1. Swarm Plots

What is a Swarm Plot?

A swarm plot is a categorical scatter plot where points are positioned to avoid overlap. It ensures each data point remains visible while preserving category alignment, making it a great tool for visualizing individual observations.

Syntax:

```
import seaborn as sns
import matplotlib.pyplot as plt
data = sns.load_dataset('tips')
sns.swarmplot(x='day', y='total_bill', hue='sex',
data=data)
plt.show()
```

Syntax Explanation:

- **sns.swarmplot(x='day', y='total_bill', hue='sex', data=data)**: Creates a swarm plot where total_bill values are distributed along the x-axis (day), with color differentiation by gender.
- **plt.show()**: Ensures the plot is displayed properly.

Example:

```
sns.swarmplot(x='sex', y='tip', hue='time', data=data)
plt.show()
```

Example Explanation:

- **hue='time'**: Differentiates meal times (Lunch/Dinner) using color.
- **Useful for understanding tipping behavior across genders and times of day.**

2. Strip Plots

What is a Strip Plot?

A strip plot is a categorical scatter plot that places all observations along a category axis, often with slight jittering to improve visibility. It is a simple way to display raw data points.

Syntax:

```
sns.stripplot(x='day', y='total_bill', data=data,
jitter=True)
plt.show()
```

Syntax Explanation:

- **sns.stripplot(x='day', y='total_bill', data=data, jitter=True)**: Creates a strip plot where total_bill values are plotted along the categorical x-axis (day), with jitter added to prevent overplotting.
- **plt.show()**: Displays the plot.

Example:

```
sns.stripplot(x='sex', y='tip', hue='smoker',
data=data, dodge=True)
plt.show()
```

Example Explanation:

- **hue='smoker'**: Differentiates smokers and non-smokers using color.
- **dodge=True**: Separates overlapping points by category.
- **Useful for analyzing tipping patterns based on smoking habits.**

3. Customizing Swarm and Strip Plots

What is Customizing Swarm and Strip Plots?
Customization allows for better clarity, improved aesthetics, and easier interpretation of swarm and strip plots. Seaborn provides options to adjust color, marker size, jitter, and category separation to make these visualizations more effective.

Syntax:
```
sns.set_style('whitegrid')
sns.swarmplot(x='day', y='total_bill', hue='sex',
data=data, palette='coolwarm')
plt.show()
```

Syntax Explanation:
- **sns.set_style('whitegrid')**: Applies a clean white grid background for enhanced readability.
- **sns.swarmplot(x='day', y='total_bill', hue='sex', data=data, palette='coolwarm')**: Creates a swarm plot with color differentiation based on gender.
- **plt.show()**: Ensures the plot is displayed correctly.

Example:
```
sns.stripplot(x='day', y='total_bill', data=data,
jitter=True, palette='muted')
plt.show()
```

Example Explanation:
- **palette='muted'**: Uses a subtle color scheme for improved contrast.
- **jitter=True**: Introduces slight movement to prevent point overlap.
- **Improves visualization clarity, making individual observations more distinguishable.**

4. Create Strip Plot

What is a Strip Plot?

A strip plot is a categorical scatter plot that represents individual data points along a categorical axis. Unlike a swarm plot, strip plots allow overlapping points unless jittering is applied. This type of plot is useful when analyzing raw data distribution within categories.

Syntax:

```
sns.stripplot(x='day', y='total_bill', data=data,
jitter=True)
plt.show()
```

Syntax Explanation:

- **`sns.stripplot(x='day', y='total_bill', data=data, jitter=True)`**: Creates a strip plot where `total_bill` values are plotted along the categorical x-axis (day), with jitter applied to prevent excessive overlap.
- **`plt.show()`**: Displays the plot and ensures visibility.

Example:

```
sns.stripplot(x='sex', y='tip', hue='smoker',
data=data, dodge=True)
plt.show()
```

Example Explanation:

- **`hue='smoker'`**: Differentiates smokers and non-smokers using color coding.
- **`dodge=True`**: Separates overlapping points into distinct groups for better clarity.
- **Useful for understanding tipping trends across different smoker statuses.**

Real-World Project: Analyzing Tipping Behavior
Project Overview:

This project explores tipping behavior using swarm and strip plots to understand how various factors influence tipping amounts. By visualizing individual tipping data points, we can identify patterns based on day, gender, smoking status, and time of the meal.

Steps:

1. **Load and preprocess the dataset** to ensure data is clean and ready for visualization.
2. **Create a swarm plot** to display individual tipping patterns across different days.
3. **Create a strip plot** to analyze raw tipping data distribution, ensuring jitter is applied for better readability.
4. **Customize the plots** with color palettes, legend adjustments, and marker sizing to improve clarity.
5. **Save and present findings** for analysis and reporting.

Example Code:

```python
import seaborn as sns
import matplotlib.pyplot as plt

data = sns.load_dataset('tips')

# Set style
sns.set_style('whitegrid')

# Swarm Plot
plt.figure(figsize=(8, 6))
sns.swarmplot(x='day', y='tip', hue='sex', data=data)
plt.title("Swarm Plot of Tips by Day and Gender")
plt.show()

# Strip Plot
plt.figure(figsize=(8, 6))
sns.stripplot(x='day', y='tip', hue='sex', data=data,
jitter=True)
plt.title("Strip Plot of Tips by Day and Gender")
plt.show()
```

Expected Result:

Swarm Plot

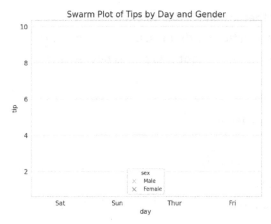

Strip Plot

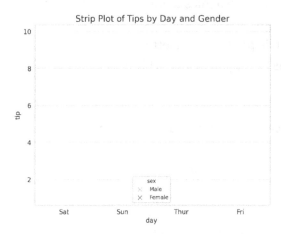

- **Swarm Plot:** Clearly visualizes tipping behavior, preventing overlap while showing individual data points.
- **Strip Plot:** Displays raw data points along the categorical axis, helping identify tipping trends.
- **Customization:** Enhances readability by using color differentiation and jittering to avoid excessive overlap.
- **Saved Plots:** Can be used for further data analysis and business insights.

Chapter 10: Styling Plots with Seaborn Themes

Seaborn provides a variety of themes and styles to enhance the appearance of plots. By applying different themes, users can improve readability, aesthetics, and clarity. This chapter explores how to use Seaborn's built-in styles, color palettes, and contextual settings to customize visualizations effectively.

Key Characteristics of Seaborn Themes:

- **Seaborn Styles:**
    - Predefined styles such as `darkgrid`, `whitegrid`, `dark`, `white`, and `ticks`.
    - Helps improve the appearance of plots with minimal effort.
- **Color Palettes:**
    - Customizable color schemes to differentiate data categories.
    - Options include predefined palettes (`deep`, `muted`, `bright`, `pastel`, `dark`, `colorblind`) and user-defined palettes.
- **Context Settings:**
    - Adjust the scale of elements (`paper`, `notebook`, `talk`, `poster`).
    - Controls the size of fonts, labels, and other visual elements.

Basic Rules for Styling Plots in Seaborn:

- **Choose an appropriate style** based on the dataset and presentation needs.
- **Use color palettes** to distinguish categories effectively.
- **Apply context settings** for different output formats (e.g., presentations vs. reports).
- **Combine themes, color palettes, and contexts** for professional-looking visualizations.
- **Ensure visual clarity and readability** by avoiding excessive styling.

Syntax Table:

SL No	Function	Syntax Example	Description
1	Import Seaborn	`import seaborn as sns`	Imports the Seaborn library.
2	Set Style	`sns.set_style('darkgrid')`	Applies a predefined style to the plot.
3	Set Color Palette	`sns.set_palette('pastel')`	Uses a predefined color palette.
4	Set Context	`sns.set_context('talk')`	Adjusts plot elements for different contexts.
5	Show Plot	`plt.show()`	Displays the customized plot.

1. Seaborn Styles

What are Seaborn Styles?

Seaborn provides five built-in styles that modify the overall appearance of plots. These styles enhance the visual clarity of data without requiring extensive manual adjustments.

Syntax:

```
import seaborn as sns
import matplotlib.pyplot as plt

data = sns.load_dataset('tips')
sns.set_style('whitegrid')
sns.scatterplot(x='total_bill', y='tip', data=data)
plt.show()
```

Syntax Explanation:

- **sns.set_style('whitegrid')**: Applies a clean grid-based background for better readability.
- **sns.scatterplot(x='total_bill', y='tip', data=data)**: Creates a scatter plot while utilizing the selected theme.
- **plt.show()**: Displays the customized plot.

Example:
```
sns.set_style('darkgrid')
sns.lineplot(x='day', y='total_bill', data=data)
plt.show()
```

Example Explanation:
- **`sns.set_style('darkgrid')`**: Uses a darker background with a grid for improved contrast.
- **Useful when presenting data with multiple lines or trends.**

2. Color Palettes

What are Color Palettes?
Color palettes allow users to apply predefined or custom colors to plots, improving visual differentiation between categories.

Syntax:
```
sns.set_palette('muted')
sns.barplot(x='day', y='total_bill', hue='sex',
data=data)
plt.show()
```

Syntax Explanation:
- **`sns.set_palette('muted')`**: Applies a softer color scheme suitable for categorical data.
- **`sns.barplot(x='day', y='total_bill', hue='sex', data=data)`**: Creates a bar plot while applying the selected color palette.
- **Improves categorical distinction and enhances readability.**

Example:
```
sns.set_palette('pastel')
sns.boxplot(x='day', y='total_bill', hue='sex',
data=data)
plt.show()
```

Example Explanation:
- **`sns.set_palette('pastel')`**: Uses a light color scheme ideal for presentations.
- **Enhances data separation while maintaining an aesthetically pleasing visualization.**

3. Context Settings

What are Context Settings?
Seaborn's context settings adjust the scale of plot elements to match different presentation needs, such as print reports, slides, and posters.
Syntax:
```
sns.set_context('poster')
sns.lineplot(x='day', y='total_bill', data=data)
plt.show()
```

Syntax Explanation:
- **sns.set_context('poster')**: Increases text and marker sizes for better readability in large-format presentations.
- **Helps in adjusting plots dynamically for different viewing needs.**

Example:
```
sns.set_context('notebook')
sns.histplot(data['total_bill'], bins=20)
plt.show()
```

Example Explanation:
- **sns.set_context('notebook')**: Optimizes the plot for viewing in coding environments.
- **Ensures that text elements and axes remain appropriately sized for analysis.**

4. Set Context

What are Context Settings?
Seaborn's context settings adjust the overall scaling of plot elements to match different presentation needs. By setting an appropriate context, users can ensure that text sizes, marker sizes, and other visual elements are proportionate for reports, presentations, or interactive analysis.
Syntax:
```
sns.set_context('poster')
sns.lineplot(x='day', y='total_bill', data=data)
plt.show()
```

Syntax Explanation:

- `sns.set_context('poster')`: Increases the size of all plot elements for better readability in large-format displays.
- `sns.lineplot(x='day', y='total_bill', data=data)`: Generates a line plot optimized for the selected context.
- **Useful for improving visibility in posters, presentations, and large-scale reports.**

Example:

```
sns.set_context('notebook')
sns.histplot(data['total_bill'], bins=20)
plt.show()
```

Example Explanation:

- `sns.set_context('notebook')`: Optimizes the plot for standard notebook displays, ensuring balanced text and marker sizes.
- **Ensures clarity and ease of reading in coding environments and data exploration workflows.**

Real-World Project: Enhancing Data Visualizations

This project explores the impact of styling options in Seaborn by applying different themes, color palettes, and context settings to improve visualization clarity and presentation.

Steps:

1. **Load and explore the dataset** to understand the available data.
2. **Apply different Seaborn styles** to see how they affect visual representation.
3. **Use color palettes** to differentiate categories within the dataset.
4. **Adjust context settings** for different display needs (e.g., reports, presentations).
5. **Save and present findings** by exporting the customized plots.

Example Code:

```python
import seaborn as sns
import matplotlib.pyplot as plt

data = sns.load_dataset('tips')

# Apply Styling
sns.set_style('whitegrid')
sns.set_palette('deep')
sns.set_context('talk')

# Create Plot
plt.figure(figsize=(8,6))
sns.scatterplot(x='total_bill', y='tip', hue='sex',
data=data)
plt.title("Styled Scatter Plot of Tips")
plt.show()
```

Expected Result:

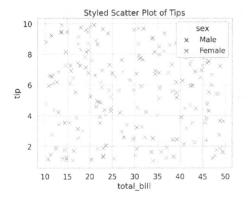

- **Styled Plot:** Uses a combination of themes, colors, and contexts to enhance clarity.
- **Improved Readability:** Ensures elements are well-spaced and easily interpretable.
- **Customization for Different Use Cases:** Optimizes plots for reports, presentations, and interactive environments.

Chapter 11: Adding Titles, Labels, and Legends in Seaborn

Titles, labels, and legends are essential components of data visualizations. They provide context, improve readability, and help users interpret plots effectively. Seaborn offers built-in functions to customize these elements, ensuring clarity and professional presentation. This chapter explores how to add and modify titles, labels, and legends in Seaborn plots.

Key Characteristics of Titles, Labels, and Legends:

- **Titles:**
  - Provide a summary of the visualization's purpose.
  - Improve plot interpretability and professionalism.
- **Labels:**
  - Identify axes and data points for better understanding.
  - Ensure numerical and categorical data are well-defined.
- **Legends:**
  - Differentiate categories using colors and markers.
  - Improve multi-variable comparisons in a single plot.

Basic Rules for Adding Titles, Labels, and Legends:

- **Use clear and descriptive titles** that summarize the plot's message.
- **Label both x and y axes** to specify numerical and categorical relationships.
- **Place the legend appropriately** to avoid clutter.
- **Customize font sizes and styles** to match presentation needs.
- **Ensure consistency across multiple visualizations** for a professional look.

Syntax Table:

SL No	Function	Syntax Example	Description
1	Add Title	`plt.title('Plot Title')`	Sets the title of the plot.
2	Add X-Label	`plt.xlabel('X-Axis Label')`	Labels the x-axis.
3	Add Y-Label	`plt.ylabel('Y-Axis Label')`	Labels the y-axis.
4	Customize Legend	`plt.legend(title='Legend Title')`	Adds a legend with a title.
5	Show Plot	`plt.show()`	Displays the final visualization.

1. Adding Titles

What is a Title?

A title provides a summary of the plot's purpose. It enhances readability and helps viewers understand the key insights of the visualization.

Syntax:

```
import seaborn as sns
import matplotlib.pyplot as plt
data = sns.load_dataset('tips')
sns.scatterplot(x='total_bill', y='tip', data=data)
plt.title('Total Bill vs. Tip Amount')
plt.show()
```

Syntax Explanation:

- **`plt.title('Total Bill vs. Tip Amount')`**: Adds a title summarizing the relationship between the plotted variables.
- **`plt.show()`**: Displays the styled plot with a title.

Example:

```
sns.histplot(data['total_bill'], bins=20)
plt.title('Distribution of Total Bills')
plt.show()
```

Example Explanation:

- **Provides a meaningful title** that describes the histogram's purpose.
- **Ensures the visualization is clear and informative.**

2. Adding Labels

What are Labels?

Labels define what each axis represents, ensuring clarity and preventing misinterpretation.

Syntax:

```
sns.boxplot(x='day', y='total_bill', data=data)
plt.xlabel('Day of the Week')
plt.ylabel('Total Bill Amount ($)')
plt.show()
```

Syntax Explanation:

- **plt.xlabel('Day of the Week')**: Labels the x-axis with categorical values.
- **plt.ylabel('Total Bill Amount ($)')**: Labels the y-axis with numerical values.
- **plt.show()**: Displays the labeled plot.

Example:

```
sns.lineplot(x='day', y='tip', data=data)
plt.xlabel('Day')
plt.ylabel('Average Tip ($)')
plt.show()
```

Example Explanation:

- **Clearly defines what each axis represents.**
- **Helps users quickly interpret numerical relationships.**

3. Customizing Legends

What is a Legend?

A legend provides information about different categories within a visualization. It helps users differentiate data groups based on colors and markers.

Syntax:

```
sns.scatterplot(x='total_bill', y='tip', hue='sex',
data=data)
plt.legend(title='Customer Gender')
plt.show()
```

Syntax Explanation:

- **hue='sex'**: Uses color to differentiate data points by gender.
- **plt.legend(title='Customer Gender')**: Adds a descriptive title to the legend.
- **plt.show()**: Ensures the final plot is rendered correctly.

Example:

```
sns.barplot(x='day', y='total_bill', hue='time',
data=data)
plt.legend(title='Meal Type', loc='upper left')
plt.show()
```

Example Explanation:

- **title='Meal Type'**: Clarifies what the legend represents.
- **loc='upper left'**: Positions the legend to avoid overlapping data.
- **Enhances plot interpretability without cluttering the visualization.**

4. Customizing Legends Further

Seaborn allows fine-tuning of legends to improve clarity and aesthetics. Users can position legends, adjust marker sizes, change fonts, and modify transparency to enhance visualization.

Syntax:

```
sns.scatterplot(x='total_bill', y='tip', hue='sex',
data=data)
plt.legend(title='Customer Gender', loc='upper left',
fontsize=12, frameon=True)
plt.show()
```

Syntax Explanation:

- **title='Customer Gender'**: Labels the legend appropriately.
- **loc='upper left'**: Positions the legend to avoid overlapping data.
- **fontsize=12**: Adjusts text size for readability.
- **frameon=True**: Adds a border around the legend for better separation.

Example:

```
sns.barplot(x='day', y='total_bill', hue='time',
data=data)
plt.legend(title='Meal Type', loc='lower right',
framealpha=0.7, fancybox=True)
plt.show()
```

Example Explanation:

- **loc='lower right'**: Places the legend at the bottom right corner.
- **framealpha=0.7**: Makes the legend background slightly transparent.
- **fancybox=True**: Rounds the legend box edges for a polished look.
- **Enhances visual appeal while maintaining clarity.**

Real-World Project: Enhancing Readability with Titles, Labels, and Legends

This project demonstrates how adding titles, labels, and legends enhances the readability of Seaborn plots. By properly labeling elements, we ensure that viewers can quickly and accurately interpret visualizations.

Steps:

1. **Load and explore the dataset.**
2. **Create a scatter plot** with meaningful titles and labels.
3. **Add a legend** to differentiate categories.
4. **Customize fonts and positions** for clarity.
5. **Save and present the findings.**

Example Code:

```
import seaborn as sns
import matplotlib.pyplot as plt
data = sns.load_dataset('tips')
# Create Scatter Plot with Title, Labels, and Legend
sns.scatterplot(x='total_bill', y='tip', hue='sex',
data=data)
plt.title('Scatter Plot of Total Bill vs. Tip')
plt.xlabel('Total Bill Amount ($)')
plt.ylabel('Tip Amount ($)')
plt.legend(title='Customer Gender')
plt.show()
```

Expected Result:

Scatter Plot with Titles, Labels, and Legends

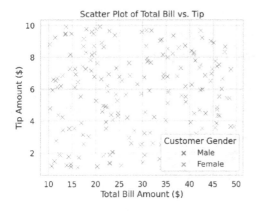

- **Well-Labeled Plot:** Clearly defined axes and an informative title.
- **Enhanced Readability:** A well-placed legend that differentiates categories.
- **Professional Presentation:** Ready-to-use visualization for reports and presentations.

Chapter 12: Customizing Axes and Grids in Seaborn

Customizing axes and grids in Seaborn improves data readability and enhances visual clarity. Axes define the scale, labels, and tick marks of a plot, while grids provide a structured background that aids interpretation. This chapter explores how to modify these elements effectively to create polished and professional-looking visualizations.

Key Characteristics of Axes and Grids:

- **Axes Customization:**
    - Control axis labels, limits, and tick marks.
    - Adjust scale types (linear, log, etc.).
    - Rotate and format tick labels.
- **Grid Customization:**
    - Toggle grid visibility for better readability.
    - Adjust line styles, colors, and spacing.
    - Apply different grid settings for major and minor ticks.

Basic Rules for Customizing Axes and Grids:

- **Ensure axes labels are clear and concise.**
- **Modify axis limits** to focus on relevant data ranges.
- **Use grid lines strategically** to improve plot readability.
- **Format tick labels properly** for better presentation.
- **Maintain consistency across multiple plots** for uniformity.

Syntax Table:

SL No	Function	Syntax Example	Description
1	Set X-Label	`plt.xlabel('X-Axis Label')`	Labels the x-axis.
2	Set Y-Label	`plt.ylabel('Y-Axis Label')`	Labels the y-axis.
3	Set Axis Limits	`plt.xlim(0, 50)`	Sets the range of x-axis values.
4	Rotate Ticks	`plt.xticks(rotation=45)`	Rotates tick labels.

5	Enable Grid	`plt.grid(True, linestyle='--')`	Displays a dashed grid.

1. Customizing Axes

What are Axes?

Axes define the scale and boundaries of a plot, providing reference points for interpreting data. Customizing them enhances clarity and ensures accurate representation of values.

Syntax:

```
import seaborn as sns
import matplotlib.pyplot as plt

data = sns.load_dataset('tips')
sns.boxplot(x='day', y='total_bill', data=data)
plt.xlabel('Day of the Week')
plt.ylabel('Total Bill Amount ($)')
plt.xticks(rotation=45)
plt.show()
```

Syntax Explanation:

- **plt.xlabel('Day of the Week')**: Adds a descriptive label to the x-axis.
- **plt.ylabel('Total Bill Amount ($)')**: Labels the y-axis with appropriate units.
- **plt.xticks(rotation=45)**: Rotates x-axis labels for better readability.
- **plt.show()**: Displays the customized plot.

Example:

```
sns.lineplot(x='total_bill', y='tip', data=data)
plt.xlim(5, 50)
plt.ylim(0, 10)
plt.xlabel('Total Bill ($)')
plt.ylabel('Tip Amount ($)')
plt.show()
```

Example Explanation:

- **`plt.xlim(5, 50)`**: Focuses the x-axis on the relevant data range.
- **`plt.ylim(0, 10)`**: Limits the y-axis to improve data visualization.
- **Improves interpretability by removing unnecessary whitespace.**

2. Customizing Grids

What are Grids?

Grids provide visual structure to a plot, making it easier to compare values. Customizing grid properties improves readability without overwhelming the visualization.

Syntax:

```
sns.histplot(data['total_bill'], bins=20)
plt.grid(True, linestyle='--', alpha=0.7)
plt.show()
```

Syntax Explanation:

- **`plt.grid(True, linestyle='--', alpha=0.7)`**: Displays a dashed grid with reduced opacity.
- **Improves value comparison without distracting from data points.**

Example:

```
sns.scatterplot(x='total_bill', y='tip', data=data)
plt.grid(True, linestyle=':', linewidth=0.8)
plt.show()
```

Example Explanation:

- **Uses a dotted grid** to subtly guide the eye without dominating the visualization.
- **Maintains plot aesthetics while improving reference lines.**

3. Customizing Axis Ticks and Labels

Why Customize Tick Labels?
Tick labels provide reference points for interpreting values. Customizing them improves clarity and presentation.

Syntax:
```
sns.boxplot(x='day', y='total_bill', data=data)
plt.xticks(rotation=30, fontsize=12)
plt.yticks(fontsize=10)
plt.show()
```

Syntax Explanation:
- **plt.xticks(rotation=30, fontsize=12)**: Rotates x-axis labels by 30 degrees and increases font size.
- **plt.yticks(fontsize=10)**: Adjusts y-axis tick label size for readability.
- **Enhances legibility without distorting the plot.**

Example:
```
sns.violinplot(x='day', y='total_bill', data=data)
plt.xticks(fontsize=14, color='blue')
plt.show()
```

Example Explanation:
- **Modifies font size and color** to enhance readability and aesthetics.
- **Improves clarity while maintaining a visually appealing design.**

4. Rotate Ticks

Rotating tick labels helps improve readability, especially when dealing with long categorical names or overlapping labels.

Syntax:
```
plt.xticks(rotation=45)
plt.yticks(rotation=30)
```

Syntax Explanation:

- **`plt.xticks(rotation=45)`**: Rotates x-axis tick labels by 45 degrees.
- **`plt.yticks(rotation=30)`**: Rotates y-axis tick labels by 30 degrees.
- **Improves label clarity without affecting the data representation.**

Example:

```
sns.barplot(x='day', y='total_bill', data=data)
plt.xticks(rotation=45, fontsize=12)
plt.show()
```

Example Explanation:

- **`fontsize=12`**: Increases font size for better visibility.
- **Rotated labels prevent overlap and enhance readability.**

5. Enable Grid

Gridlines help guide the viewer's eye along the data, making it easier to compare values across categories.

Syntax:

```
plt.grid(True, linestyle='--', alpha=0.5)
```

Syntax Explanation:

- **`plt.grid(True)`**: Enables gridlines on the plot.
- **`linestyle='--'`**: Uses a dashed grid style for subtlety.
- **`alpha=0.5`**: Sets grid transparency to reduce visual clutter.

Example:

```
sns.lineplot(x='total_bill', y='tip', data=data)
plt.grid(True, linestyle=':', linewidth=0.8)
plt.show()
```

Example Explanation:

- **Uses dotted gridlines** to enhance the visual structure without distraction.
- **Ensures alignment of data points across the plot.**

Real-World Project: Improving Visualization Readability

This project demonstrates how customizing axes and grids improves readability and presentation quality.

Steps:

1. **Load and explore the dataset.**
2. **Apply axis customizations** to improve label positioning and readability.
3. **Adjust tick labels** for better clarity.
4. **Use grids effectively** to aid data interpretation.
5. **Save and present the findings.**

Example Code:

```
import seaborn as sns
import matplotlib.pyplot as plt

data = sns.load_dataset('tips')

# Apply Customizations
sns.lineplot(x='total_bill', y='tip', data=data)
plt.xlabel('Total Bill ($)')
plt.ylabel('Tip Amount ($)')
plt.xlim(5, 50)
plt.xticks(rotation=30, fontsize=12)
plt.grid(True, linestyle='--', alpha=0.5)
plt.show()
```

Expected Result: Custom Axes and Grid Plot

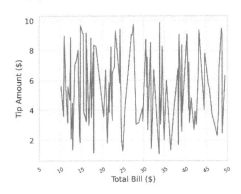

Chapter 13: Working with Palettes for Color Customization

Color customization in Seaborn enhances data visualization by improving readability and differentiating categories. Seaborn provides various color palettes, allowing users to choose predefined schemes or create custom palettes. This chapter explores how to work with different color palettes to create visually appealing and effective plots.

Key Characteristics of Seaborn Palettes:

- **Predefined Palettes:**
  - ○ Includes options like deep, muted, bright, pastel, dark, and colorblind.
  - ○ Ensures effective category differentiation.
- **Custom Palettes:**
  - ○ Allows users to define specific colors.
  - ○ Supports RGB, HEX, and named color formats.
- **Diverging and Sequential Palettes:**
  - ○ Useful for visualizing gradients and distributions.
  - ○ Includes coolwarm, rocket, magma, and viridis palettes.

Basic Rules for Using Color Palettes:

- **Choose a palette that enhances clarity** without overwhelming the viewer.
- **Use categorical palettes** for discrete variables.
- **Use sequential palettes** for numerical data.
- **Apply diverging palettes** when highlighting positive and negative values.
- **Ensure colorblind-friendly palettes** for accessibility.

Syntax Table:

SL No	Function	Syntax Example	Description
1	Set Color Palette	`sns.set_palette('pastel')`	Applies a predefined color scheme.

2	Use Custom Palette	`sns.color_palette(['#FF5733', '#33FF57'])`	Defines a custom palette using HEX colors.
3	Apply Palette to Plot	`sns.barplot(x='day', y='total_bill', hue='sex', data=data, palette='muted')`	Uses a palette in a specific plot.
4	Use Diverging Palette	`sns.diverging_palette(220, 20, as_cmap=True)`	Generates a gradient for continuous data.
5	Show Color Palette	`sns.palplot(sns.color_palette('deep'))`	Displays the selected color scheme.

1. Using Predefined Palettes
What are Predefined Palettes?
Predefined palettes provide ready-to-use color schemes for categorical and numerical data.
Syntax:
```
import seaborn as sns
import matplotlib.pyplot as plt

data = sns.load_dataset('tips')
sns.set_palette('pastel')
sns.barplot(x='day', y='total_bill', hue='sex',
data=data)
plt.show()
```
Syntax Explanation:
- **`sns.set_palette('pastel')`**: Applies a soft color palette.
- **`sns.barplot(...)`**: Uses the selected palette to color the bars.
- **Ensures clarity and enhances visual appeal.**

Example:
```
sns.set_palette('bright')
sns.boxplot(x='day', y='total_bill', hue='sex',
data=data)
plt.show()
```

Example Explanation:

- Uses a vibrant color palette for high contrast.
- Improves differentiation between categories.

2. Creating Custom Palettes

What are Custom Palettes?
Custom palettes allow users to define their own color schemes for plots.
Syntax:
```
custom_palette = sns.color_palette(['#FF5733',
'#33FF57', '#3357FF'])
sns.set_palette(custom_palette)
sns.scatterplot(x='total_bill', y='tip', hue='sex',
data=data)
plt.show()
```
Syntax Explanation:

- **sns.color_palette([...])**: Defines a custom color list using HEX codes.
- Ensures unique and personalized color schemes.

Example:
```
sns.set_palette(['#FFDD44', '#44DDEE', '#DD44AA'])
sns.violinplot(x='day', y='total_bill', hue='sex',
data=data)
plt.show()
```
Example Explanation:

- Applies a manually selected color scheme to the plot.
- Provides flexibility for branding and specific visual themes.

3. Using Diverging and Sequential Palettes

What are Diverging and Sequential Palettes?
These palettes are used for visualizing continuous numerical data with gradients.
Syntax:
```
sns.heatmap(data.corr(), cmap='coolwarm', annot=True)
plt.show()
```

Syntax Explanation:

- **cmap='coolwarm'**: Applies a diverging palette for highlighting positive and negative values.
- **Ideal for correlation matrices and continuous value representation.**

Example:
```
sns.heatmap(data.pivot_table(index='day',
columns='sex', values='total_bill'), cmap='magma',
annot=True)
plt.show()
```

Example Explanation:

- **Uses the magma colormap for better contrast in heatmaps.**
- **Enhances interpretation of numerical distributions.**

4. Using Diverging Palettes

Diverging palettes are useful when visualizing continuous data with both positive and negative values, allowing distinct emphasis on extremes.

Syntax:
```
sns.heatmap(data.corr(),
cmap=sns.diverging_palette(220, 20, as_cmap=True),
annot=True)
plt.show()
```

Syntax Explanation:

- **sns.diverging_palette(220, 20, as_cmap=True)**: Creates a diverging color gradient.
- **cmap='coolwarm'**: Uses a predefined diverging colormap.
- **Highlights variations in correlation matrices and continuous data.**

Example:
```
sns.heatmap(data.pivot_table(index='day',
columns='sex', values='total_bill'),
cmap=sns.diverging_palette(145, 280, as_cmap=True),
annot=True)
plt.show()
```

Example Explanation:
- **Applies a custom diverging palette** to differentiate positive and negative variations.
- **Enhances interpretation of numerical trends.**

5. Displaying a Color Palette

Seaborn allows users to visualize color palettes before applying them to plots.

Syntax:
```
sns.palplot(sns.color_palette('pastel'))
```

Syntax Explanation:
- **sns.palplot(sns.color_palette('pastel'))**: Displays the pastel color palette.
- **Useful for previewing palettes before applying them to plots.**

Example:
```
sns.palplot(sns.color_palette(['#FF5733', '#33FF57', '#3357FF']))
```

Example Explanation:
- **Displays a custom palette** to ensure color choices align with visualization needs.
- **Helps in selecting color themes for branding or presentation consistency.**

Real-World Project: Enhancing Data Visualization with Color

This project demonstrates how color palettes improve visual distinction and presentation.

Steps:
1. **Load and explore the dataset.**
2. **Apply different predefined palettes** to compare their effectiveness.
3. **Use a custom palette** for personalized visualization.
4. **Apply a sequential palette** to enhance numerical data

interpretation.

5. Save and present the findings.

Example Code:

```python
import seaborn as sns
import matplotlib.pyplot as plt

data = sns.load_dataset('tips')

# Apply Custom Palette
sns.set_palette('muted')
sns.barplot(x='day', y='total_bill', hue='sex',
data=data)
plt.title("Bar Plot with Muted Palette")
plt.show()

# Apply Sequential Palette
sns.heatmap(data.pivot_table(index='day',
columns='sex', values='total_bill'), cmap='viridis',
annot=True)
plt.title("Heatmap with Sequential Palette")
plt.show()
```

Expected Result:

Predefined Palette

Sequential Palette Heatmap

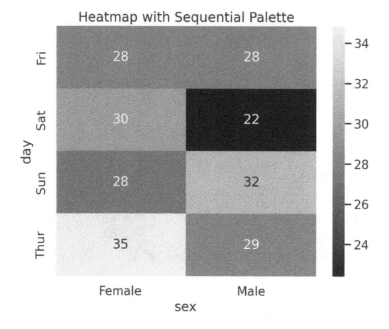

- **Categorical Plots:** Improved differentiation between groups.
- **Heatmaps:** Enhanced contrast for better interpretation.
- **Custom Color Themes:** Allows personalized visual storytelling.

Chapter 14: Pair Plots for Multivariate Data Analysis

Pair plots are a fundamental tool in multivariate data analysis, allowing users to explore relationships between multiple variables in a dataset. Seaborn's `pairplot()` function makes it easy to create pairwise scatterplots and histograms, helping identify patterns, trends, and potential correlations. This chapter covers how to use pair plots effectively for exploratory data analysis.

Key Characteristics of Pair Plots:

- **Displays pairwise relationships** between numerical variables.
- **Includes diagonal histograms or KDE plots** for univariate distributions.
- **Supports categorical differentiation** using the hue parameter.
- **Provides an overview of data distribution** and relationships in a dataset.

Basic Rules for Using Pair Plots:

- **Use pair plots for datasets with numerical variables.**
- **Apply the hue parameter** to visualize categorical group differences.
- **Adjust markers and colors** for better readability in large datasets.
- **Customize diagonal plots** to display histograms or KDEs for univariate analysis.
- **Use subset filtering** to focus on relevant relationships.

Syntax Table:

SL No	Function	Syntax Example	Description
1	Create Pair Plot	`sns.pairplot(data)`	Generates pairwise scatterplots and histograms.
2	Add Hue (Categorical)	`sns.pairplot(data, hue='species')`	Differentiates categories using color.

3	Customize Diagonal Plot	`sns.pairplot(data, diag_kind='kde')`	Uses KDE instead of histograms on the diagonal.
4	Set Specific Variables	`sns.pairplot(data, vars=['bill_length _mm', 'flipper_length_mm '])`	Plots only selected variables.
5	Adjust Markers	`sns.pairplot(data, hue='species', markers=['o', 's', 'D'])`	Uses different markers for categories.

1. Creating Basic Pair Plots

What is a Pair Plot?

A pair plot visualizes relationships between multiple numerical variables by plotting scatter plots for pairwise comparisons and histograms for univariate distributions.

Syntax:

```
import seaborn as sns
import matplotlib.pyplot as plt
data = sns.load_dataset('penguins')
sns.pairplot(data)
plt.show()
```

Syntax Explanation:

- **sns.pairplot(data)**: Generates scatter plots for each numerical variable combination and histograms for individual variables.
- **Helps identify relationships and trends in multivariate datasets.**

Example:

```
sns.pairplot(data, vars=['bill_length_mm',
'bill_depth_mm', 'flipper_length_mm'])
plt.show()
```

Example Explanation:

- **Focuses on specific variables** to reduce clutter in large datasets.
- **Allows a more detailed analysis of selected feature relationships.**

2. Using Hue for Categorical Differentiation

What is Hue in Pair Plots?
The hue parameter categorizes data points by color, making it easier to compare different groups within the dataset.
Syntax:
```
sns.pairplot(data, hue='species')
plt.show()
```

Syntax Explanation:
- **hue='species'**: Colors scatter plots based on species, helping visualize group differences.
- **Enhances multivariate analysis by distinguishing categorical groups.**

Example:
```
sns.pairplot(data, hue='sex', markers=['o', 's'])
plt.show()
```

Example Explanation:
- **Uses different markers (o*************************, s)** for male and female categories.
- **Improves data distinction in overlapping clusters.**

3. Customizing Diagonal Plots

What are Diagonal Plots in Pair Plots?
Diagonal plots display univariate distributions. By default, they show histograms but can be customized to use kernel density estimation (KDE) plots.
Syntax:
```
sns.pairplot(data, diag_kind='kde')
plt.show()
```
Syntax Explanation:
- **diag_kind='kde'**: Uses KDE plots instead of histograms for smoother distributions.
- **Provides a clearer view of density variations.**

Example:
```
sns.pairplot(data, hue='species', diag_kind='kde')
plt.show()
```

Example Explanation:
- **Combines hue differentiation with KDE for enhanced insights.**
- **Shows how distributions vary across categorical groups.**

4. Set Specific Variables

Pair plots can become cluttered when too many variables are included. To focus on specific relationships, users can define a subset of variables for visualization.

Syntax:
```
sns.pairplot(data, vars=['bill_length_mm',
'flipper_length_mm'])
plt.show()
```

Syntax Explanation:
- **vars=['bill_length_mm', 'flipper_length_mm']**: Limits the pair plot to only the specified numerical columns.
- **Reduces clutter and improves analysis of key relationships.**

Example:
```
sns.pairplot(data, vars=['bill_length_mm',
'bill_depth_mm', 'body_mass_g'])
plt.show()
```

Example Explanation:
- **Focuses only on selected numerical features for detailed exploration.**
- **Helps avoid unnecessary comparisons in large datasets.**

5. Adjust Markers

To improve clarity in categorical differentiation, users can customize the markers used for each category in a pair plot.

Syntax:
```
sns.pairplot(data, hue='species', markers=['o', 's',
'D'])
plt.show()
```

Syntax Explanation:
- **hue='species'**: Differentiates species by color.
- **markers=['o', 's', 'D']**: Assigns unique markers to each species to improve visual separation.
- **Useful when analyzing overlapping points.**

Example:
```
sns.pairplot(data, hue='sex', markers=['^', 'v'])
plt.show()
```

Example Explanation:
- **Uses triangle markers (^******** for males, v for females) for better category distinction.**
- **Enhances visual differentiation in dense scatter plots.**

Real-World Project: Exploring Penguin Species Data

This project demonstrates how pair plots help analyze species differences using the penguins dataset.

Steps:
1. **Load and explore the dataset.**
2. **Generate a basic pair plot** to examine variable relationships.
3. **Use the hue parameter** to differentiate species visually.
4. **Customize diagonal plots** to display KDE distributions.
5. **Analyze patterns** and potential correlations between features.

Example Code:
```
import seaborn as sns
import matplotlib.pyplot as plt

data = sns.load_dataset('penguins')
# Pair Plot with Hue and KDE Diagonal
sns.pairplot(data, hue='species', diag_kind='kde')
plt.show()
```

Expected Result:

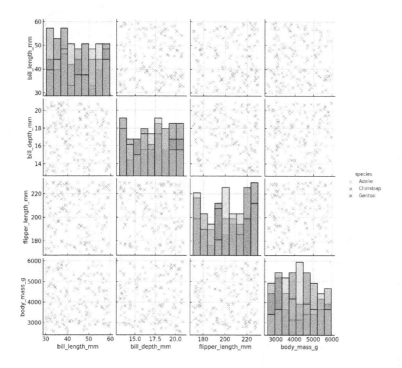

- **Multivariate Analysis:** Shows relationships between numerical variables.
- **Categorical Differentiation:** Uses color coding to distinguish species.
- **Univariate Distributions:** Displays KDE plots for better density insights.
- **Professional Presentation:** A clean, well-organized visualization for analysis.

Chapter 15: Heatmaps for Correlation and Matrix Visualization

Heatmaps are a powerful tool for visualizing relationships between numerical variables in a dataset. Seaborn's `heatmap()` function allows users to display correlation matrices and other structured data in a color-coded format, making it easier to identify patterns, trends, and outliers. This chapter covers how to create and customize heatmaps effectively for data analysis.

Key Characteristics of Heatmaps:
- **Displays numerical relationships** using color intensity.
- **Commonly used for correlation matrices** in exploratory data analysis.
- **Customizable color palettes** for better readability and interpretation.
- **Supports annotations** for precise value representation.
- **Handles missing data effectively** with visual indicators.

Basic Rules for Using Heatmaps:
- **Use heatmaps to explore numerical relationships.**
- **Apply correlation matrices** to understand feature interactions.
- **Customize color palettes** for clear differentiation of values.
- **Enable annotations** for easier data interpretation.
- **Ensure proper scaling and formatting** to avoid misleading visualizations.

Syntax Table:

SL No	Function	Syntax Example	Description
1	Create Heatmap	`sns.heatmap(data.corr())`	Generates a correlation heatmap.
2	Add Annotations	`sns.heatmap(data.corr(), annot=True)`	Displays correlation values inside the heatmap.
3	Customize Color Palette	`sns.heatmap(data.corr(), cmap='coolwarm')`	Applies a diverging color palette.

4	Adjust Value Scaling	`sns.heatmap(data.corr(), vmin=-1, vmax=1)`	Sets min and max color scale.
5	Mask Upper Triangle	`sns.heatmap(corr, mask=np.triu(corr))`	Hides redundant half of the matrix.

1. Creating a Basic Heatmap

What is a Heatmap?

A heatmap is a visualization tool that uses color to represent values in a matrix. It is commonly used for analyzing correlation between numerical features in a dataset.

Syntax:

```
import seaborn as sns
import matplotlib.pyplot as plt
import numpy as np

data = sns.load_dataset('penguins')
corr_matrix = data.corr()
sns.heatmap(corr_matrix)
plt.show()
```

Syntax Explanation:

- **data.corr()**: Computes the correlation matrix of numerical variables.
- **sns.heatmap(corr_matrix)**: Creates a heatmap from the correlation matrix.
- **Helps identify strong or weak correlations between features.**

Example:

```
sns.heatmap(corr_matrix, annot=True)
plt.show()
```

Example Explanation:

- **Enables annotations (annot=True************************)** to display numerical values inside the heatmap.
- **Improves interpretability of the correlation strengths.**

2. Customizing Heatmaps with Color Palettes

What are Heatmap Color Palettes?
Seaborn provides various color palettes to differentiate values effectively in heatmaps.

Syntax:
```
sns.heatmap(corr_matrix, cmap='coolwarm')
plt.show()
```

Syntax Explanation:
- **cmap='coolwarm'**: Uses a diverging color palette to highlight positive and negative correlations.
- **Enhances contrast for better data analysis.**

Example:
```
sns.heatmap(corr_matrix, cmap='magma', annot=True)
plt.show()
```

Example Explanation:
- **Applies the magma color map for high-contrast visualization.**
- **Annotations improve numerical clarity within the heatmap.**

3. Masking Upper Triangle for Clarity

Why Mask the Upper Triangle?
Since correlation matrices are symmetric, displaying both halves is redundant. Masking the upper triangle improves readability.

Syntax:
```
mask = np.triu(np.ones_like(corr_matrix, dtype=bool))
sns.heatmap(corr_matrix, mask=mask, annot=True)
plt.show()
```

Syntax Explanation:
- **np.triu(np.ones_like(corr_matrix, dtype=bool))**: Creates a mask for the upper triangle.
- **mask=mask**: Hides redundant values to declutter the heatmap.

Example:
```
sns.heatmap(corr_matrix, mask=mask, cmap='coolwarm',
annot=True)
plt.show()
```

Example Explanation:
- **Removes duplicate information from the heatmap.**
- **Improves visualization focus by displaying only necessary values.**

4. Adjust Value Scaling

Value scaling ensures that the heatmap colors accurately represent the range of values in the dataset. By defining minimum and maximum values, users can control color contrast and avoid misleading visualizations.

Syntax:
```
sns.heatmap(corr_matrix, vmin=-1, vmax=1,
cmap='coolwarm', annot=True)
plt.show()
```

Syntax Explanation:
- `vmin=-1, vmax=1`: Sets the range of values displayed in the heatmap, ensuring consistent interpretation of colors.
- `cmap='coolwarm'`: Uses a diverging color palette to highlight correlations effectively.
- **Avoids misleading extreme values affecting color scaling.**

Example:
```
sns.heatmap(corr_matrix, vmin=0, vmax=1, cmap='Blues',
annot=True)
plt.show()
```

Example Explanation:

- **Limits values to between 0 and 1 for positive correlations only.**
- **Uses a sequential palette (Blues****) to show increasing strength of relationships.**

5. Mask Upper Triangle

Since correlation matrices are symmetrical, showing both halves can be redundant. Masking the upper triangle removes duplicated information and enhances readability.

Syntax:
```
mask = np.triu(np.ones_like(corr_matrix, dtype=bool))
sns.heatmap(corr_matrix, mask=mask, annot=True,
cmap='coolwarm')
plt.show()
```

Syntax Explanation:
- **np.triu(np.ones_like(corr_matrix, dtype=bool)):** Creates a mask to hide the upper triangle of the correlation matrix.
- **mask=mask**: Applies the mask, removing duplicate correlations.
- **Improves clarity by displaying only necessary data.**

Example:
```
mask = np.triu(np.ones_like(corr_matrix, dtype=bool))
sns.heatmap(corr_matrix, mask=mask, cmap='magma',
annot=True)
plt.show()
```

Example Explanation:
- **Uses the magma colormap for better contrast.**
- **Enhances focus on key correlations without redundant data.**

Real-World Project: Exploring Feature Correlations in Penguins Dataset

This project demonstrates how heatmaps help analyze correlations between penguin species attributes.

Steps:
1. **Load and preprocess the dataset.**
2. **Generate a basic correlation heatmap.**
3. **Customize the heatmap color palette for better readability.**
4. **Mask the upper triangle** to reduce redundancy.
5. **Analyze relationships between features.**

Example Code:

```
import seaborn as sns
import matplotlib.pyplot as plt
import numpy as np

data = sns.load_dataset('penguins')
corr_matrix = data.corr()

# Mask upper triangle
mask = np.triu(np.ones_like(corr_matrix, dtype=bool))

# Create Heatmap with Customization
sns.heatmap(corr_matrix, mask=mask, cmap='coolwarm',
annot=True)
plt.title("Correlation Heatmap of Penguin Features")
plt.show()
```

Expected Result:

Correlation Heatmap

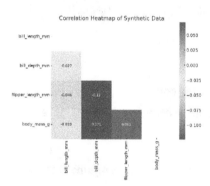

- **Clear Visualization of Correlations:** Helps identify relationships between features.
- **Custom Color Palettes:** Highlights positive and negative correlations effectively.
- **Masked Upper Triangle:** Reduces visual clutter for better interpretation.
- **Professional Presentation:** Provides insights for data analysis and decision-making.

Chapter 16: Facet Grids for Complex Subplots

Facet grids allow users to create multiple subplots based on categorical variables, making it easier to analyze relationships across different groups. Seaborn's `FacetGrid` and `catplot` functions provide a structured way to visualize complex multivariate data. This chapter explores how to create, customize, and interpret facet grids in Seaborn.

Key Characteristics of Facet Grids:

- **Enables multi-panel visualizations** based on categorical grouping.
- **Helps identify patterns across subsets of data.**
- **Works well with scatter, line, bar, and KDE plots.**
- **Allows customization of layout, size, and labels.**
- **Facilitates efficient comparisons across multiple categories.**

Basic Rules for Using Facet Grids:

- **Choose appropriate categorical variables** for faceting.
- **Ensure enough data points** in each facet for meaningful analysis.
- **Use proper axis labeling** to avoid misinterpretation.
- **Apply consistent styles and color palettes** for clarity.
- **Limit the number of facets** to prevent excessive complexity.

Syntax Table:

SL No	Function	Syntax Example	Description
1	Create FacetGrid	`g = sns.FacetGrid(data, col='species')`	Creates a grid of subplots based on a category.
2	Map a Plot Type	`g.map(sns.scatterplot, 'bill_length_mm', 'bill_depth_mm')`	Maps a scatter plot to each facet.
3	Customize Labels	`g.set_axis_labels('X Label', 'Y Label')`	Sets axis labels for clarity.
4	Adjust Layout	`g.set_titles(col_template='{col_name}')`	Formats titles for each subplot.

5	Use catplot	`sns.catplot(x='sex', y='body_mass_g', col='species', kind='box', data=data)`	Creates a categorical facet plot.

1. Creating Basic Facet Grids

What is a Facet Grid?

A facet grid is a multi-panel plot where each subplot visualizes data for a specific category, making it easier to compare trends and distributions across multiple groups.

Syntax:

```
import seaborn as sns
import matplotlib.pyplot as plt
data = sns.load_dataset('penguins')
g = sns.FacetGrid(data, col='species')
g.map(sns.scatterplot, 'bill_length_mm',
'bill_depth_mm')
plt.show()
```

Syntax Explanation:

- **`sns.FacetGrid(data, col='species')`**: Creates subplots for each penguin species.
- **`g.map(sns.scatterplot, 'bill_length_mm', 'bill_depth_mm')`**: Plots a scatter plot for each facet.
- **Helps visualize species-specific patterns in bill measurements.**

Example:

```
g = sns.FacetGrid(data, col='island', hue='species')
g.map(sns.kdeplot, 'body_mass_g', fill=True)
g.add_legend()
plt.show()
```

Example Explanation:

- **Facets are based on the island category.**
- **Different species are color-coded for better distinction.**
- **KDE plots highlight the distribution of body mass within each island.**

2. Using catplot for Categorical Faceting

What is catplot?
`catplot` is a high-level function that simplifies the creation of facet grids for categorical plots like boxplots, bar plots, and violin plots.

Syntax:
```
sns.catplot(x='sex', y='body_mass_g', col='species',
kind='box', data=data)
plt.show()
```

Syntax Explanation:
- **kind='box'**: Creates boxplots for each species.
- **Facets columns by species, allowing easy comparison.**
- **Useful for categorical comparisons across multiple groups.**

Example:
```
sns.catplot(x='day', y='total_bill', col='sex',
kind='bar', data=sns.load_dataset('tips'))
plt.show()
```

Example Explanation:
- **Compares tipping behavior by day and gender.**
- **Uses bar plots to visualize mean differences in total bill.**

3. Customizing Facet Grids

Why Customize Facet Grids?
Customizing facet grids improves clarity, enhances readability, and ensures consistency in presentations.

Syntax:
```
g.set_axis_labels('Bill Length (mm)', 'Bill Depth
(mm)')
g.set_titles(col_template='{col_name} Island')
g.fig.suptitle('Penguin Species Comparison',
fontsize=16)
plt.show()
```

Syntax Explanation:
- **set_axis_labels()**: Sets axis labels for all facets.
- **set_titles()**: Customizes the subplot titles.
- **fig.suptitle()**: Adds a global title to the facet grid.

Example:

```
g = sns.FacetGrid(data, col='species')
g.map_dataframe(sns.histplot, x='body_mass_g')
g.set_axis_labels('Body Mass (g)', 'Frequency')
g.set_titles(col_template='Species: {col_name}')
plt.show()
```

Example Explanation:
- **Creates histogram plots for body mass across species.**
- **Improves clarity with custom labels and titles.**

4. Adjust Layout

Customizing the layout of facet grids ensures readability and better data presentation. Users can adjust the number of rows, columns, aspect ratios, and spacing between plots.

Syntax:

```
g = sns.FacetGrid(data, col='species', col_wrap=2,
height=4, aspect=1.2)
g.map(sns.scatterplot, 'bill_length_mm',
'bill_depth_mm')
plt.show()
```

Syntax Explanation:
- **col_wrap=2**: Limits the number of columns in the grid, wrapping additional plots to the next row.
- **height=4**: Sets the height of each subplot.
- **aspect=1.2**: Adjusts the width-to-height ratio for better visualization.
- **Improves clarity by managing plot layout effectively.**

Example:

```
g = sns.FacetGrid(data, col='species', height=5,
despine=False)
g.map_dataframe(sns.histplot, x='body_mass_g',
kde=True)
g.set_titles(col_template='Species: {col_name}')
plt.show()
```

Example Explanation:
- **Larger plot size enhances visibility.**
- **Histogram with KDE provides a clear density estimate.**
- **Custom titles ensure easy identification of categories.**

5. Use catplot

Seaborn's `catplot` function simplifies categorical faceting by combining facet grids with category-based plots like boxplots and bar plots.
Syntax:
```
sns.catplot(x='sex', y='body_mass_g', col='species',
kind='box', height=4, aspect=1.2, data=data)
plt.show()
```

Syntax Explanation:
- **`kind='box'`**: Creates boxplots for comparing distributions across categories.
- **`height=4, aspect=1.2`**: Adjusts subplot size for better readability.
- **Provides a structured way to analyze categorical variations.**

Example:
```
sns.catplot(x='day', y='total_bill', col='sex',
kind='bar', height=5, aspect=1,
data=sns.load_dataset('tips'))
plt.show()
```

Example Explanation:
- **Analyzes tipping behavior across days, separated by gender.**
- **Bar plots clearly show mean values for comparison.**
- **Custom sizing improves visualization without crowding the layout.**

Real-World Project: Analyzing Penguin Traits Across Species

This project demonstrates how facet grids help analyze variations in penguin species traits.

Steps:

1. **Load and explore the dataset.**
2. **Generate a scatter plot facet grid** to analyze bill dimensions.
3. **Use a KDE plot facet grid** to examine body mass distributions.
4. Apply categorical faceting with catplot to explore sex-based differences.
5. **Customize the facet grid layout** for better readability.

Example Code:

```
import seaborn as sns
import matplotlib.pyplot as plt

data = sns.load_dataset('penguins')

# Scatter plot FacetGrid
g = sns.FacetGrid(data, col='species')
g.map(sns.scatterplot, 'bill_length_mm',
'bill_depth_mm')
g.set_axis_labels('Bill Length (mm)', 'Bill Depth
(mm)')
g.set_titles(col_template='Species: {col_name}')
plt.show()
```

Expected Result:

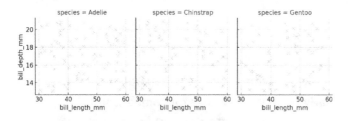

- **Multivariate Comparison:** Displays relationships across species.
- **Categorical Differentiation:** Uses colors and facets for clear segmentation.
- **Custom Labels and Titles:** Ensures clarity in visual presentation.

Chapter 17: Joint Plots for Exploring Relationships

Joint plots are a powerful tool for exploring relationships between two numerical variables while also displaying their marginal distributions. Seaborn's `jointplot()` function allows users to visualize bivariate relationships using scatter plots, regression lines, KDE plots, and histograms. This chapter explores how to use joint plots effectively to analyze variable interactions.

Key Characteristics of Joint Plots:

- **Combines bivariate and univariate visualizations** in a single plot.
- **Supports multiple plot types**, including scatter, regression, KDE, and histograms.
- **Helps detect trends, correlations, and distributions** between two variables.
- **Customizable with color palettes, markers, and annotations.**
- **Ideal for exploratory data analysis (EDA)** in continuous datasets.

Basic Rules for Using Joint Plots:

- **Choose two numerical variables** to compare relationships effectively.
- **Use scatter or regression plots** for linear relationships.
- **Apply KDE plots** to examine density distributions.
- **Ensure adequate data points** for reliable interpretation.
- **Customize color palettes and styles** for better readability.

Syntax Table:

SL No	Function	Syntax Example	Description
1	Create Basic Joint Plot	`sns.jointplot(x='bill_length_mm', y='bill_depth_mm', data=data)`	Generates a scatter plot with marginal histograms.
2	Add Regression Line	`sns.jointplot(x='total_bill', y='tip', data=data, kind='reg')`	Displays a scatter plot with a regression line.

3	Use KDE for Density	```sns.jointplot(x='flip per_length_mm', y='body_mass_g', data=data, kind='kde')```	Generates density contours for both variables.
4	Customize Appearance	```sns.jointplot(x='bill _length_mm', y='bill_depth_mm', data=data, hue='species', palette='coolwarm')```	Uses color coding for categorical differentiation.
5	Adjust Marginal Plots	```sns.jointplot(x='tota l_bill', y='tip', data=data).plot_margi nals(sns.kdeplot, color='r')```	Customizes the marginal plots.

1. Creating a Basic Joint Plot

What is a Joint Plot?
A joint plot visualizes the relationship between two numerical variables while displaying their marginal distributions.

Syntax:
```
import seaborn as sns
import matplotlib.pyplot as plt

data = sns.load_dataset('penguins')
sns.jointplot(x='bill_length_mm', y='bill_depth_mm',
data=data)
plt.show()
```

Syntax Explanation:
- **sns.jointplot(x='bill_length_mm', y='bill_depth_mm', data=data)**: Creates a scatter plot with marginal histograms.
- **Helps analyze relationships and variable distributions simultaneously.**

Example:
```
sns.jointplot(x='flipper_length_mm', y='body_mass_g',
data=data)
plt.show()
```

Example Explanation:
- Visualizes body mass in relation to flipper length.
- Scatter plot reveals clustering patterns in the data.

2. Using Regression Lines in Joint Plots

What is a Regression Joint Plot?
Adding a regression line to a joint plot helps visualize trends and correlations between two numerical variables.
Syntax:
```
sns.jointplot(x='total_bill', y='tip',
data=sns.load_dataset('tips'), kind='reg')
plt.show()
```

Syntax Explanation:
- **kind='reg'**: Adds a linear regression line to show trend direction.
- Scatter points illustrate data dispersion.

Example:
```
sns.jointplot(x='bill_length_mm', y='body_mass_g',
data=data, kind='reg')
plt.show()
```

Example Explanation:
- Displays a regression trend between bill length and body mass.
- Regression slope helps identify correlation strength.

3. Visualizing Density with KDE Joint Plots

What is a KDE Joint Plot?
Kernel Density Estimation (KDE) joint plots display density distributions for both numerical variables.
Syntax:
```
sns.jointplot(x='flipper_length_mm', y='body_mass_g',
data=data, kind='kde')
plt.show()
```

Syntax Explanation:
- **kind='kde'**: Generates a smooth density contour plot.
- **Highlights regions of high and low data density.**

Example:
```
sns.jointplot(x='bill_length_mm', y='bill_depth_mm',
data=data, kind='kde')
plt.show()
```

Example Explanation:
- **Shows density variations between bill length and depth.**
- **Useful for analyzing distributions in continuous datasets.**

4. Customize Appearance

Customizing joint plots enhances readability and allows differentiation between categories using colors, markers, and labels.
Syntax:
```
sns.jointplot(x='bill_length_mm', y='bill_depth_mm',
data=data, hue='species', palette='coolwarm')
plt.show()
```

Syntax Explanation:
- **hue='species'**: Differentiates data points by species color.
- **palette='coolwarm'**: Uses a predefined color scheme to enhance clarity.
- **Improves categorical distinction within joint plots.**

Example:
```
sns.jointplot(x='total_bill', y='tip',
data=sns.load_dataset('tips'), hue='sex',
palette='Set2')
plt.show()
```

Example Explanation:
- Uses the Set2 color palette for gender differentiation.
- Enhances plot interpretability with clear categorical separation.

5. Adjust Marginal Plots

Marginal plots display univariate distributions for each variable.
Customizing these plots helps highlight data patterns more effectively.
Syntax:
```
sns.jointplot(x='total_bill', y='tip',
data=sns.load_dataset('tips')).plot_marginals(sns.kdepl
ot, color='r')
plt.show()
```

Syntax Explanation:
- **plot_marginals(sns.kdeplot, color='r')**: Replaces default histograms with KDE plots in red.
- **Provides smoother representations of variable distributions.**

Example:
```
sns.jointplot(x='bill_length_mm', y='bill_depth_mm',
data=data).plot_marginals(sns.histplot, bins=20,
color='g')
plt.show()
```

Example Explanation:
- Uses green-colored histograms with 20 bins for detailed distribution analysis.
- Improves visualization clarity while maintaining data precision.

Real-World Project: Exploring Bill Dimensions in Penguins

This project demonstrates how joint plots help analyze the relationships between penguin bill dimensions and body mass.

Steps:

1. **Load and preprocess the dataset.**
2. **Generate a basic joint plot** to explore variable relationships.
3. **Use regression analysis** to examine trends between bill length and mass.
4. **Apply KDE plots** to highlight density variations.
5. **Customize the visualization** with color palettes and annotations.

Example Code:

```
import seaborn as sns
import matplotlib.pyplot as plt
data = sns.load_dataset('penguins')
# Scatter Joint Plot with KDE
sns.jointplot(x='bill_length_mm', y='bill_depth_mm',
data=data, kind='kde')
plt.show()
```

Expected Result:

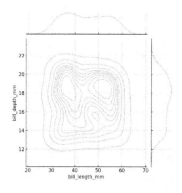

- **Visual Relationship Analysis:** Displays correlations between numerical variables.
- **Trend Identification:** Regression lines help understand variable dependencies.
- **Enhanced Readability:** KDE plots provide density insights.
- **Professional Presentation:** Ensures clear and informative data storytelling.

Chapter 18: Regression Plots with Seaborn

Regression plots are a fundamental tool for visualizing relationships between two numerical variables while adding regression lines to indicate trends. Seaborn's `regplot()` and `lmplot()` functions provide a clear way to represent correlations and fit regression models. This chapter explores how to use regression plots effectively to analyze trends in data.

Key Characteristics of Regression Plots:

- **Shows linear relationships** between two numerical variables.
- **Adds a regression line** with confidence intervals.
- **Supports scatter points overlay** for better pattern recognition.
- **Customizable with hue, markers, and polynomial fits.**
- **Useful for trend analysis and predictive modeling.**

Basic Rules for Using Regression Plots:

- Use `regplot()` for simple regression visualization.
- Apply `lmplot()` for categorical faceting and comparisons.
- **Ensure numerical variables** are suitable for regression analysis.
- **Customize colors, confidence intervals, and scatter markers.**
- **Use polynomial fits** for nonlinear relationships if needed.

Syntax Table:

SL No	Function	Syntax Example	Description
1	Create Basic Regression Plot	`sns.regplot(x='tot al_bill', y='tip', data=data)`	Generates a scatter plot with a regression line.
2	Add Categorical Hue	`sns.lmplot(x='tota l_bill', y='tip', hue='sex', data=data)`	Differentiates categories by color.
3	Remove Confidence Interval	`sns.regplot(x='fli pper_length_mm', y='body_mass_g', data=data, ci=None)`	Removes shaded confidence interval.

4	Use Polynomial Regression	`sns.regplot(x='bil l_length_mm', y='bill_depth_mm', data=data, order=2)`	Fits a second-degree polynomial regression.
5	Facet Data with Implot	`sns.lmplot(x='tota l_bill', y='tip', col='sex', data=data)`	Creates separate plots for each category.

1. Creating a Basic Regression Plot

What is a Regression Plot?
A regression plot visualizes the relationship between two numerical variables while adding a regression line to highlight trends.

Syntax:
```
import seaborn as sns
import matplotlib.pyplot as plt

data = sns.load_dataset('tips')
sns.regplot(x='total_bill', y='tip', data=data)
plt.show()
```

Syntax Explanation:
- **`sns.regplot(x='total_bill', y='tip', data=data)`**: Creates a scatter plot with a regression line.
- **Regression line helps visualize trend direction and strength.**

Example:
```
sns.regplot(x='flipper_length_mm', y='body_mass_g', data=sns.load_dataset('penguins'))
plt.show()
```

Example Explanation:
- **Displays the relationship between flipper length and body mass.**
- **Regression line shows an increasing trend.**

2. Using lmplot for Categorical Faceting

What is an Implot?
lmplot extends regression visualization by allowing categorical faceting.
Syntax:
```
sns.lmplot(x='total_bill', y='tip', hue='sex',
data=data)
plt.show()
```

Syntax Explanation:
- **hue='sex'**: Differentiates male and female customers by color.
- **Allows categorical comparison in regression analysis.**

Example:
```
sns.lmplot(x='bill_length_mm', y='bill_depth_mm',
col='species', data=sns.load_dataset('penguins'))
plt.show()
```

Example Explanation:
- **Facets plots by penguin species to compare trends.**
- **Provides separate regression analyses for each species.**

3. Customizing Regression Plots

Why Customize Regression Plots?
Customization improves clarity and allows better differentiation of trends.
Syntax:
```
sns.regplot(x='total_bill', y='tip', data=data,
ci=None, scatter_kws={'color':'r'})
plt.show()
```

Syntax Explanation:
- **ci=None**: Removes confidence intervals for a cleaner plot.
- **scatter_kws={'color':'r'}**: Colors scatter points red for better contrast.

Example:

```
sns.regplot(x='flipper_length_mm', y='body_mass_g',
data=sns.load_dataset('penguins'), color='g')
plt.show()
```

Example Explanation:
- Uses green for better contrast.
- Removes confidence interval for a focused trend line.

4. Use Polynomial Regression

Polynomial regression can be useful for capturing nonlinear trends in data. By increasing the polynomial order, users can fit more complex relationships.

Syntax:

```
sns.regplot(x='bill_length_mm', y='bill_depth_mm',
data=data, order=2)
plt.show()
```

Syntax Explanation:
- **order=2**: Fits a second-degree polynomial regression line.
- **Captures nonlinear trends** in the relationship between variables.

Example:

```
sns.regplot(x='total_bill', y='tip',
data=sns.load_dataset('tips'), order=3, ci=None)
plt.show()
```

Example Explanation:
- Uses a third-degree polynomial fit for more complex trends.
- Removes confidence intervals (ci=None) for a cleaner view.

5. Facet Data with Implot

Faceting allows users to compare regression trends across different categories by splitting the data into multiple subplots.

Syntax:

```
sns.lmplot(x='total_bill', y='tip', col='sex',
data=data)
plt.show()
```

Syntax Explanation:
- **col='sex'**: Creates separate regression plots for male and female customers.
- **Useful for category-based trend analysis.**

Example:

```
sns.lmplot(x='bill_length_mm', y='bill_depth_mm',
col='species', hue='species',
data=sns.load_dataset('penguins'))
plt.show()
```

Example Explanation:
- **Facets regression plots by penguin species.**
- **Allows visual comparison of regression trends across species.**

Real-World Project: Analyzing Tip Trends in Restaurants

This project demonstrates how regression plots help analyze tipping behavior in restaurants.

Steps:
1. **Load and preprocess the dataset.**
2. **Generate a basic regression plot** to explore tip trends.
3. **Use categorical faceting** to compare trends by gender.
4. **Customize confidence intervals and colors** for better clarity.
5. **Interpret findings based on regression trends.**

Example Code:

```
import seaborn as sns
import matplotlib.pyplot as plt
data = sns.load_dataset('tips')

# Basic Regression Plot
sns.regplot(x='total_bill', y='tip', data=data,
color='b')
plt.show()
```

Expected Result:

- **Trend Identification:** Regression lines help understand tipping behavior.
- **Categorical Comparison:** Faceted plots differentiate trends by gender.
- **Custom Visual Enhancements:** Improves plot readability and analysis.

Chapter 19: Time Series Visualization in Seaborn

Time series visualization helps track changes in data over time, allowing users to identify trends, seasonality, and patterns. Seaborn provides tools like `lineplot()` to create effective time series plots. This chapter explores how to visualize and analyze time-based data using Seaborn.

Key Characteristics of Time Series Visualization:

- **Displays trends and fluctuations** over a continuous time scale.
- **Useful for forecasting and pattern recognition.**
- **Supports multiple time-dependent variables** in a single plot.
- **Customizable with markers, colors, and line styles.**
- **Can be combined with rolling averages and smoothing techniques.**

Basic Rules for Using Time Series Plots:

- **Ensure time data is properly formatted** (datetime format recommended).
- **Use `lineplot()` for smooth trend visualization.**
- **Apply rolling averages** to smooth fluctuations.
- **Differentiate categories** using color or hue parameter.
- **Label axes properly** to ensure clear interpretation.

Syntax Table:

SL No	Function	Syntax Example	Description
1	Create Line Plot	`sns.lineplot(x='date', y='value', data=data)`	Generates a basic time series plot.
2	Add Hue for Category	`sns.lineplot(x='date', y='value', hue='category', data=data)`	Differentiates categories using color.
3	Apply Rolling Mean	`data['rolling_avg'] = data['value'].rolling(7).mean()`	Computes a moving average for trend analysis.

		sns.lineplot(x='da te', y='value', data=data, linestyle='--')	
4	Customize Appearance	sns.lineplot(x='da te', y='value', data=data, linestyle='--')	Adjusts line styles for emphasis.
5	Set Time Format	plt.xticks(rotatio n=45)	Rotates x-axis labels for better readability.

1. Creating a Basic Time Series Plot

What is a Time Series Plot?

A time series plot visualizes changes in a numerical variable over time, helping identify trends and seasonal effects.

Syntax:

```
import seaborn as sns
import matplotlib.pyplot as plt
import pandas as pd
# Create sample data
data = pd.DataFrame({'date': pd.date_range(start='2023-01-01', periods=100, freq='D'),
                    'value':
np.random.rand(100).cumsum()})

# Plot time series
data['date'] = pd.to_datetime(data['date'])
sns.lineplot(x='date', y='value', data=data)
plt.xticks(rotation=45)
plt.show()
```

Syntax Explanation:

- **pd.date_range()**: Generates a sequence of dates.
- **sns.lineplot()**: Creates a time series plot.
- **plt.xticks(rotation=45)**: Rotates date labels for readability.

Example:

```
sns.lineplot(x='date', y='value', data=data, color='b')
plt.show()
```

Example Explanation:
- **Visualizes numerical trends over time.**
- **Customizes color for better clarity.**

2. Using Hue to Differentiate Categories

What is Hue in Time Series Plots?
The hue parameter allows differentiation between multiple time series using distinct colors.

Syntax:
```
sns.lineplot(x='date', y='value', hue='category',
data=data)
plt.show()
```

Syntax Explanation:
- **hue='category'**: Differentiates data series using colors.
- **Useful for comparing multiple groups over time.**

Example:
```
sns.lineplot(x='date', y='value', hue='region',
style='region', data=data)
plt.show()
```

Example Explanation:
- **Distinguishes regions with color and line style.**
- **Enhances interpretability for multiple time series.**

3. Applying Rolling Averages

What is a Rolling Average?
A rolling average smooths short-term fluctuations, making long-term trends clearer.

Syntax:
```
data['rolling_avg'] = data['value'].rolling(7).mean()
sns.lineplot(x='date', y='rolling_avg', data=data)
plt.show()
```

Syntax Explanation:
- **`rolling(7).mean()`**: Computes a 7-day moving average.
- **Smooths out noise in time series data.**

Example:
```
sns.lineplot(x='date', y='rolling_avg', data=data,
linestyle='--', color='r')
plt.show()
```

Example Explanation:
- **Uses dashed lines for better distinction.**
- **Emphasizes long-term trends in the data.**

4. Customize Appearance

Customizing the appearance of time series plots improves clarity and readability. Users can modify line styles, colors, markers, and background settings to enhance data visualization.

Syntax:
```
sns.lineplot(x='date', y='value', data=data,
linestyle='--', marker='o', color='b')
plt.show()
```

Syntax Explanation:
- **`linestyle='--'`**: Uses dashed lines for better visual separation.
- **`marker='o'`**: Adds circular markers to indicate data points.
- **`color='b'`**: Changes the line color to blue.

Example:
```
sns.lineplot(x='date', y='value', data=data,
linewidth=2, linestyle='-', marker='s', color='g')
plt.show()
```

Example Explanation:
- **Uses thicker lines (`linewidth=2`) for better visibility.**
- **Applies square markers (`marker='s'`) to highlight individual data points.**
- **Ensures better contrast with green color.**

5. Set Time Format

Properly formatting time labels ensures readability, especially when dealing with extensive time series data.

Syntax:
```
plt.xticks(rotation=45, fontsize=12)
plt.gca().xaxis.set_major_formatter(plt.matplotlib.date
s.DateFormatter('%b %Y'))
```

Syntax Explanation:
- **plt.xticks(rotation=45, fontsize=12)**: Rotates labels for readability and increases font size.
- **plt.gca().xaxis.set_major_formatter(plt.matplotli b.dates.DateFormatter('%b %Y'))**: Formats the date labels to show month and year.

Example:
```
import matplotlib.dates as mdates
plt.xticks(rotation=30)
plt.gca().xaxis.set_major_locator(mdates.MonthLocator()
)
plt.gca().xaxis.set_major_formatter(mdates.DateFormatte
r('%Y-%m'))
plt.show()
```

Example Explanation:
- Uses **MonthLocator()** to display only one label per month.
- Formats date labels as **YYYY-MM** for better clarity in long-term trends.
- **Enhances time series visualization when working with large datasets.**

Real-World Project: Analyzing Website Traffic Trends

This project demonstrates how time series visualization helps analyze website traffic trends.

Steps:

1. **Load and preprocess the dataset.**
2. **Generate a basic time series plot** to explore traffic fluctuations.
3. **Use the hue parameter** to differentiate traffic sources.
4. **Apply rolling averages** to highlight trends.
5. **Interpret findings based on seasonal variations.**

Example Code:

```
import seaborn as sns
import matplotlib.pyplot as plt
import pandas as pd
import numpy as np


# Create synthetic website traffic data
data = pd.DataFrame({'date': pd.date_range(start='2023-
01-01', periods=100, freq='D'),
                     'visits': np.random.randint(500,
2000, size=100)})
data['rolling_avg'] = data['visits'].rolling(7).mean()


# Plot Time Series with Rolling Average
sns.lineplot(x='date', y='visits', data=data,
label='Daily Visits')
sns.lineplot(x='date', y='rolling_avg', data=data,
linestyle='--', color='r', label='7-Day Avg')
plt.xticks(rotation=45)
plt.legend()
plt.show()
```

Expected Result:

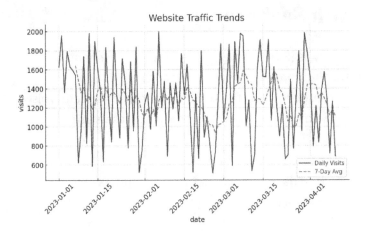

- **Trend Identification:** Shows daily fluctuations and smoothed trends.
- **Seasonal Patterns:** Highlights long-term cycles and anomalies.
- **Custom Visual Enhancements:** Improves readability with colors and line styles.

Chapter 20: Loading and Exploring Datasets with Seaborn

Exploratory Data Analysis (EDA) is an essential step in understanding datasets before visualization and modeling. Seaborn provides built-in datasets and easy-to-use functions for loading and inspecting data. This chapter explores how to load, preview, and analyze datasets using Seaborn.

Key Characteristics of Loading and Exploring Data:

- **Supports built-in datasets** such as tips, penguins, and iris.
- **Allows quick data inspection** using head(), info(), and describe().
- **Facilitates missing value detection and handling.**
- **Integrates seamlessly with Pandas for advanced analysis.**
- **Works with different file formats** (CSV, Excel, etc.) via Pandas.

Basic Rules for Loading and Exploring Data:

- Use **sns.get_dataset_names()** to view available built-in datasets.
- Apply **sns.load_dataset()** to load datasets into Pandas DataFrames.
- Use **.head()** and **.info()** to understand dataset structure.
- **Handle missing values** using dropna() or fillna().
- **Check data distributions** with .describe() and Seaborn visualization tools.

Syntax Table:

SL No	Function	Syntax Example	Description
1	List Available Datasets	sns.get_dataset _names()	Displays built-in datasets in Seaborn.
2	Load Dataset	data = sns.load_datase t('tips')	Loads a dataset into a Pandas DataFrame.
3	View Data Structure	data.info()	Prints column details and data types.
4	Preview Data	data.head()	Displays the first five

			rows.
5	Check Summary Stats	`data.describe()`	Provides statistical insights.

1. Listing and Loading Datasets

What are Built-in Datasets?
Seaborn includes built-in datasets for quick testing and demonstration of visualization techniques.

Syntax:
```
import seaborn as sns

# List available datasets
print(sns.get_dataset_names())

# Load a dataset
data = sns.load_dataset('tips')
```

Syntax Explanation:
- **sns.get_dataset_names()**: Lists all available datasets.
- **sns.load_dataset('tips')**: Loads the tips dataset into a Pandas DataFrame.
- **Useful for testing visualization functions.**

Example:
```
data = sns.load_dataset('penguins')
print(data.head())
```

Example Explanation:
- **Loads the penguins dataset and displays the first five rows.**
- **Provides a quick overview of dataset structure.**

2. Inspecting Data Structure

Why Inspect a Dataset?
Understanding the dataset structure helps in identifying missing values, data types, and feature distributions.

Syntax:
```
print(data.info())
```

Syntax Explanation:
- **data.info()**: Prints dataset column names, types, and missing values.
- **Ensures readiness for visualization and modeling.**

Example:
```
data = sns.load_dataset('iris')
print(data.info())
```

Example Explanation:
- **Displays column details, including types and null values.**
- **Helps identify potential data cleaning steps.**

3. Checking Summary Statistics

Why Use Summary Statistics?
Statistical summaries help understand data distributions and detect anomalies.

Syntax:
```
print(data.describe())
```

Syntax Explanation:
- **data.describe()**: Returns count, mean, standard deviation, and quartiles for numerical columns.
- **Useful for identifying trends and outliers.**

Example:
```
print(data.describe(include='all'))
```

Example Explanation:
- **Includes both numerical and categorical summary statistics.**
- **Shows frequency distributions for categorical variables.**

4. Preview Data

Previewing data allows users to quickly examine a dataset's structure and contents, making it easier to identify key features.

Syntax:

```
print(data.head())
print(data.tail())
```

Syntax Explanation:

- **data.head()**: Displays the first five rows of the dataset.
- **data.tail()**: Displays the last five rows of the dataset.
- **Useful for getting an initial overview of the dataset.**

Example:

```
data = sns.load_dataset('penguins')
print(data.head(10))
```

Example Explanation:

- **Loads the penguins dataset and displays the first 10 rows.**
- **Helps in understanding initial data distributions.**

5. Check Summary Stats

Checking summary statistics helps users analyze key numerical properties and detect anomalies in the dataset.

Syntax:

```
print(data.describe())
print(data.describe(include='all'))
```

Syntax Explanation:

- **data.describe()**: Returns summary statistics for numerical columns.
- **data.describe(include='all')**: Includes both numerical and categorical data summaries.
- **Useful for understanding data distributions and potential outliers.**

Example:

```
print(data.describe(percentiles=[0.1, 0.5, 0.9]))
```

Example Explanation:
- Calculates additional percentiles (10%, 50%, and 90%) for deeper insight.
- Allows a more tailored statistical summary.

Real-World Project: Exploring the Titanic Dataset

This project demonstrates how to load, inspect, and analyze the Titanic dataset using Seaborn.

Steps:
1. Load the dataset.
2. Inspect column details using .info().
3. Check missing values and handle them appropriately.
4. Use summary statistics to understand feature distributions.
5. Prepare the data for visualization and modeling.

Example Code:

```
import seaborn as sns

# Load dataset
data = sns.load_dataset('titanic')

# Inspect dataset structure
print(data.info())

# Check summary statistics
print(data.describe(include='all'))
```

Expected Result:

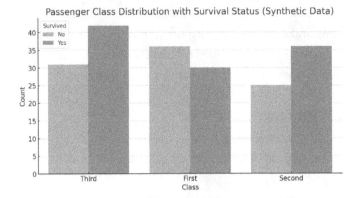

Passenger Class Distribution with Survival Status (Synthetic Data)

- **Dataset Overview:** Displays dataset structure and missing values.
- **Statistical Insights:** Summarizes key numerical and categorical features.
- **Data Cleaning Readiness:** Prepares dataset for further analysis.

Chapter 21: Handling Missing Data in Seaborn Visualizations

Handling missing data is an essential step in data preprocessing to ensure accurate visualizations and analysis. Seaborn provides built-in methods to detect, visualize, and handle missing values efficiently. This chapter explores different techniques to manage missing data in Seaborn visualizations.

Key Characteristics of Handling Missing Data:

- **Identifies missing values using Pandas functions.**
- **Visualizes missing data distribution** using Seaborn's `heatmap()` and `missingno` library.
- **Allows data cleaning with `dropna()` and `fillna()`.**
- **Ensures that missing values do not impact visualization accuracy.**
- **Supports imputation strategies** such as mean, median, or forward-filling.

Basic Rules for Handling Missing Data:

- Use `isnull().sum()` to check for missing values in the dataset.
- Apply **`dropna()`** when missing data is minimal.
- Use **`fillna()`** to replace missing values when appropriate.
- **Visualize missing values** using heatmaps to identify patterns.
- **Choose an imputation method** based on dataset characteristics.

Syntax Table:

SL No	Function	Syntax Example	Description
1	Check Missing Values	`data.isnull().sum()`	Displays count of missing values per column.
2	Drop Missing Values	`data.dropna()`	Removes rows with missing values.
3	Fill Missing Values	`data.fillna(data.mean())`	Replaces missing values with the column mean.
4	Visualize Missing Data	`sns.heatmap(data.isnull(), cbar=False, cmap='viridis')`	Displays a heatmap of missing values.

5	Use Forward Fill	`data.fillna(meth od='ffill')`	Fills missing values with the previous row's value.

1. Checking for Missing Values

What is Missing Data?
Missing data occurs when certain observations in a dataset have no recorded values, which can affect data analysis and visualization.

Syntax:
```
import seaborn as sns
import pandas as pd

# Load dataset
data = sns.load_dataset('titanic')

# Check missing values
print(data.isnull().sum())
```

Syntax Explanation:
- **`data.isnull().sum()`**: Counts missing values in each column.
- **Helps identify features with missing data for further processing.**

Example:
```
missing_values =
data.isnull().sum().sort_values(ascending=False)
print(missing_values[missing_values > 0])
```

Example Explanation:
- **Sorts columns based on missing value count.**
- **Displays only columns with missing values for focused analysis.**

2. Dropping Missing Values

What is Dropping Missing Values?
If missing values are minimal and do not significantly impact the dataset, they can be removed.

Syntax:
```
data_cleaned = data.dropna()
```

Syntax Explanation:
- **dropna()**: Removes rows containing missing values.
- **Ensures complete data for visualization and modeling.**

Example:
```
data_subset = data.dropna(subset=['age', 'fare'])
```

Example Explanation:
- **Drops rows where age or fare contain missing values.**
- **Preserves only relevant observations for analysis.**

3. Filling Missing Values

What is Data Imputation?
Instead of removing missing data, missing values can be replaced with meaningful estimates.

Syntax:
```
data_filled = data.fillna(data.mean())
```

Syntax Explanation:
- **fillna(data.mean())**: Replaces missing values with column means.
- **Prevents data loss while maintaining dataset integrity.**

Example:
```
data['age'] = data['age'].fillna(data['age'].median())
```

Example Explanation:
- **Uses median instead of mean for skewed distributions.**
- **Reduces bias caused by extreme values.**

4. Visualizing Missing Data

Why Visualize Missing Data?
A missing data heatmap helps identify patterns of missingness across features.
Syntax:
```
import seaborn as sns
import matplotlib.pyplot as plt

sns.heatmap(data.isnull(), cbar=False, cmap='viridis')
plt.show()
```

Syntax Explanation:
- **data.isnull()**: Converts missing values into a boolean matrix.
- **sns.heatmap()**: Highlights missing values using a heatmap.
- **Helps detect systematic missing patterns.**

Example:
```
sns.heatmap(data.isnull(), cmap='coolwarm', cbar=False)
plt.show()
```

Example Explanation:
- **Uses coolwarm color map for better contrast.**
- **Clearly visualizes missing value distrition.**

5. Using Forward Fill

Forward filling is a technique used to replace missing values by propagating the last valid observation forward.
Syntax:
```
data.fillna(method='ffill', inplace=True)
```

Syntax Explanation:
- **method='ffill'**: Fills missing values using the previous row's data.
- **Ensures that trends and patterns are maintained in sequential data.**
- **Best suited for time-series and ordered datasets.**

Example:

```
data['age'] = data['age'].fillna(method='ffill')
```

Example Explanation:
- Replaces missing age values with the last available value.
- Prevents gaps in sequential data while preserving structure.

Real-World Project: Handling Missing Data in Titanic Dataset

This project demonstrates how to handle missing values in the Titanic dataset using Seaborn.

Steps:
1. Load the dataset and check for missing values.
2. Visualize missing values using a heatmap.
3. Remove rows with excessive missing data.
4. Fill missing values using appropriate imputation techniques.
5. Re-check dataset structure after cleaning.

Example Code:

```
import seaborn as sns
import matplotlib.pyplot as plt
import pandas as pd

# Load Titanic dataset
data = sns.load_dataset('titanic')

# Visualize missing data
sns.heatmap(data.isnull(), cbar=False, cmap='coolwarm')
plt.show()

# Handle missing values
data_cleaned = data.fillna({'age':
data['age'].median(), 'embark_town': 'Unknown'})

# Verify changes
print(data_cleaned.isnull().sum())
```

Expected Result:

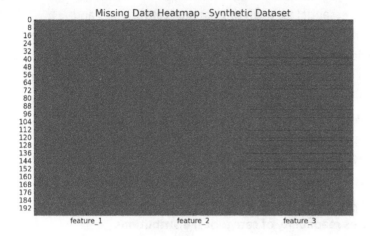

- **Identifies missing values in key features.**
- **Replaces missing values with appropriate imputation techniques.**
- **Ensures dataset is clean and ready for analysis.**

Chapter 22: Grouping Data for Categorical Analysis with Seaborn

Grouping data is essential for analyzing categorical variables and understanding relationships between different groups. Seaborn provides powerful functions such as groupby(), barplot(), and boxplot() to summarize and visualize grouped data. This chapter explores how to use Seaborn for categorical data analysis.

Key Characteristics of Grouping Data in Seaborn:
- **Facilitates comparison of categories** using summary statistics.
- **Supports aggregation functions** such as mean, count, and sum.
- **Visualizes grouped data** with bar plots, box plots, and violin plots.
- **Works well with Pandas groupby()** for data aggregation.
- **Enhances readability of categorical distributions.**

Basic Rules for Grouping Data:
- **Use groupby() to compute aggregated statistics for categories.**
- **Use barplot() for mean comparisons across categories.**
- **Apply countplot() to visualize category frequencies.**
- **Use boxplot() and violinplot() for spread and distribution analysis.**
- **Ensure categorical variables are correctly formatted.**

Syntax Table:

SL No	Function	Syntax Example	Description
1	Group Data with Pandas	data.groupby('category')['value'].mean()	Computes the mean of each category.
2	Create Bar Plot	sns.barplot(x='category', y='value', data=data)	Displays the mean value per category.
3	Count Categories	sns.countplot(x='category', data=data)	Shows the frequency of each category.
4	Box Plot for Groups	sns.boxplot(x='category', y='value', data=data)	Displays distributions for each category.

5	Violin Plot for Spread	`sns.violinplot(x='category', y='value', data=data)`	Combines density and distribution analysis.

1. Grouping Data with Pandas

What is Grouping Data?

Grouping data helps summarize and analyze categorical relationships by aggregating numerical features.

Syntax:

```
import pandas as pd
import seaborn as sns

# Load dataset
data = sns.load_dataset('tips')

# Group by categorical column
grouped_data = data.groupby('day')['total_bill'].mean()
print(grouped_data)
```

Syntax Explanation:

- **groupby('day')['total_bill'].mean()**: Computes the mean total bill per day.
- **Useful for summarizing categorical differences.**

Example:

```
grouped_data = data.groupby(['day', 'sex'])['total_bill'].sum()
print(grouped_data)
```

Example Explanation:

- **Aggregates total bill amounts based on both day and gender.**
- **Allows multi-level grouping for deeper insights.**

2. Visualizing Grouped Data with Bar Plots

What is a Bar Plot?
Bar plots display the average value of a numerical variable for each category.
Syntax:
```
sns.barplot(x='day', y='total_bill', data=data)
plt.show()
```

Syntax Explanation:
- **Displays average total bill per day.**
- **Useful for comparing category-wise means.**

Example:
```
sns.barplot(x='sex', y='tip', hue='day', data=data)
plt.show()
```

Example Explanation:
- **Groups by gender (sex*********************) and uses color coding (hue='day'*********************).**
- **Allows side-by-side comparison across days.**

3. Counting Categorical Values

What is a Count Plot?
A count plot shows the frequency of each category in a dataset.
Syntax:
```
sns.countplot(x='day', data=data)
plt.show()
```

Syntax Explanation:
- **countplot()**: Displays the count of observations for each category.
- **Useful for categorical frequency analysis.**

Example:
```
sns.countplot(x='sex', hue='day', data=data)
plt.show()
```

Example Explanation:
- **Differentiates counts based on day using hue.**
- **Shows distribution across multiple groups.**

4. Using Box Plots for Category Analysis

What is a Box Plot?
A box plot visualizes the distribution, median, and outliers of numerical values grouped by categories.

Syntax:
```
sns.boxplot(x='day', y='total_bill', data=data)
plt.show()
```

Syntax Explanation:
- **Shows spread of total bill amounts per day.**
- **Identifies outliers and variability.**

Example:
```
sns.boxplot(x='sex', y='tip', hue='day', data=data)
plt.show()
```

Example Explanation:
- **Uses hue to split data by day.**
- **Enhances category-based trend analysis.**

5. Violin Plot for Spread

What is a Violin Plot?
A violin plot combines aspects of box plots and density plots to display distributions for each category, highlighting variations and probabilities.

Syntax:
```
sns.violinplot(x='day', y='total_bill', data=data)
plt.show()
```

Syntax Explanation:

- **Combines box plot and KDE for better visualization of data distribution.**
- **Displays median, quartiles, and density estimates for each category.**

Example:

```
sns.violinplot(x='sex', y='tip', hue='day', data=data,
split=True)
plt.show()
```

Example Explanation:

- **Uses split=True to separate violin halves for better comparison.**
- **Enhances insights into the spread of tipping behavior across categories.**

Real-World Project: Analyzing Restaurant Tippi Trends

This project demonstrates how to group and analyze tipping behavior in restaurants.

Steps:

1. **Load and inspect the dataset.**
2. **Use groupby() to summarize tipping trends by day.**
3. **Visualize category distributions with count plots.**
4. **Compare means using bar plots and box plots.**
5. **Interpret findings for actionable insights.**

Example Code:

```
import seaborn as sns
import matplotlib.pyplot as plt
data = sns.load_dataset('tips')
# Bar plot to compare mean tips per day
sns.barplot(x='day', y='tip', data=data)
plt.show()
# Count plot for gender distribution
sns.countplot(x='sex', hue='day', data=data)
plt.show()
```

Expected Result:

- **Category-Based Summaries:** Computes averages and counts for categorical variables.
- **Graphical Insights:** Visualizes tipping behavior across different groups.
- **Trend Identification:** Highlights variations in tipping patterns.

Chapter 23: Using Pandas with Seaborn for Efficient Data Processing

Pandas and Seaborn complement each other for efficient data manipulation and visualization. While Pandas excels at data processing and transformation, Seaborn provides high-level visualization tools that integrate seamlessly with Pandas DataFrames. This chapter explores how to use Pandas and Seaborn together to preprocess, analyze, and visualize datasets effectively.

Key Characteristics of Using Pandas with Seaborn:

- **Facilitates seamless data manipulation** before visualization.
- **Supports grouping, aggregation, and filtering** for improved analysis.
- **Works with missing values and categorical transformations.**
- **Enables direct plotting from Pandas DataFrames.**
- **Improves efficiency in exploratory data analysis (EDA).**

Basic Rules for Using Pandas with Seaborn:

- **Use groupby() for categorical aggregations before visualization.**
- **Handle missing values with fillna() or dropna() before plotting.**
- **Use query() for efficient filtering of data.**
- **Apply melt() to restructure DataFrames for facet visualization.**
- **Leverage Pandas' datetime functions** for time-series plots.

Syntax Table:

SL No	Function	Syntax Example	Description
1	Group Data with Pandas	`data.groupby('category')['value'].mean()`	Aggregates values per category.
2	Filter Data Efficiently	`data.query("value > 50")`	Selects rows where value > 50.

3	Handle Missing Data	`data.fillna(method ='ffill')`	Replaces missing values using forward fill.
4	Transform Data for Seaborn	`data.melt(id_vars= 'category')`	Converts wide format to long format.
5	Convert Date Column	`data['date'] = pd.to_datetime(dat a['date'])`	Converts string date to datetime format.

1. Grouping and Aggregating Data

What is Data Grouping?
Grouping data helps in summarizing categorical data before visualization.
Syntax:
```
import pandas as pd
import seaborn as sns

# Load dataset
data = sns.load_dataset('tips')

# Group by categorical column
grouped_data = data.groupby('day')['total_bill'].mean()
print(grouped_data)
```

Syntax Explanation:
- **groupby('day')['total_bill'].mean()**: Computes the mean total bill per day.
- **Prepares summarized data for visualization.**

Example:
```
grouped_data = data.groupby(['day',
'sex'])['total_bill'].sum()
print(grouped_data)
```
Example Explanation:
- **Aggregates total bill values per day and gender.**
- **Allows comparison across multiple categories.**

2. Filtering Data for Analysis

What is Query Filtering?
The query() method allows filtering of DataFrames in a readable and efficient manner.
Syntax:
```
filtered_data = data.query("total_bill > 20")
print(filtered_data.head())
```

Syntax Explanation:
- **Filters rows where total bill is greater than 20.**
- **Enhances data selection before visualization.**

Example:
```
filtered_data = data.query("sex == 'Female' & tip > 5")
```

Example Explanation:
- **Selects female customers who gave tips greater than 5.**
- **Improves category-focused analysis.**

3. Handling Missing Data Before Visualization

What is Handling Missing Data?
Seaborn relies on complete datasets for accurate plots, so missing values should be addressed.
Syntax:
```
data.fillna(method='bfill', inplace=True)
```
Syntax Explanation:
- **bfill** (backfill) replaces missing values with the next available value.**
- **Ensures data integrity before visualization.**

Example:
```
data['age'] = data['age'].fillna(data['age'].median())
```

Example Explanation:
- **Uses median imputation to fill missing age values.**
- **Reduces the impact of outliers.**

4. Reshaping Data for Seaborn Visualization

Why Use Melt for Visualization?
The melt() function converts wide-format DataFrames into a long format for better visualization.

Syntax:
```
melted_data = data.melt(id_vars='day',
value_vars=['total_bill', 'tip'])
print(melted_data.head())
```

Syntax Explanation:
- Converts multiple columns into key-value pairs.
- Useful for faceted visualizations in Seaborn.

Example:
```
sns.catplot(x='day', y='value', hue='variable',
kind='bar', data=melted_data)
plt.show()
```

Example Explanation:
- Creates a grouped bar plot for total bill and tip per day.
- Allows multiple comparisons in one visualization.

5. Convert Date Column

What is Date Conversion?
Date conversion ensures that time-based data is properly formatted for time-series analysis and visualization.

Syntax:
```
data['date'] = pd.to_datetime(data['date'])
```

Syntax Explanation:
- **pd.to_datetime(data['date'])**: Converts string-based date values into datetime format.
- Facilitates time-series analysis and visualization.

Example:

```
data['order_date'] = pd.to_datetime(data['order_date'])
print(data['order_date'].dt.year.head())
```

Example Explanation:

- Converts order_date column to datetime format.
- Extracts the year component for further analysis.

Real-World Project: Analyzing Sales Trends

This project demonstrates how Pandas and Seaborn work together to analyze sales trends.

Steps:

1. Load and preprocess dataset (handling missing values, filtering, grouping).
2. Transform dataset for visualization using melt().
3. Create a bar plot comparing product sales across regions.
4. Use filtering to analyze a specific time period.
5. Visualize category distributions using Seaborn.

Example Code:

```
import seaborn as sns
import matplotlib.pyplot as plt
import pandas as pd
# Create sample dataset
data = pd.DataFrame({'region': ['North', 'South',
'East', 'West'] * 5,
                     'sales': np.random.randint(500,
2000, 20),
                     'month': ['Jan', 'Feb', 'Mar',
'Apr', 'May'] * 4})

# Bar plot for sales by region
sns.barplot(x='region', y='sales', data=data)
plt.show()
```

Expected Result:

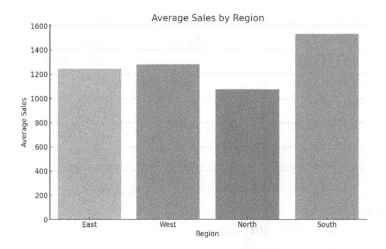

- **Efficient Data Processing:** Uses Pandas functions to clean and transform data.
- **Optimized Visualization:** Prepares structured data for Seaborn plots.
- **Actionable Insights:** Identifies regional trends in sales.

Chapter 24: Combining Seaborn with NumPy for Advanced Customizations

NumPy enhances Seaborn's visualization capabilities by providing powerful numerical operations for data transformations, statistical calculations, and customized visualizations. This chapter explores how to integrate NumPy with Seaborn to optimize data visualization.

Key Characteristics of Using NumPy with Seaborn:

- **Enables efficient numerical operations** for data transformation.
- **Facilitates advanced statistical customizations.**
- **Integrates with Seaborn for dynamic plot enhancements.**
- **Allows creation of synthetic data** for testing visualizations.
- **Supports mathematical transformations** for better insights.

Basic Rules for Using NumPy with Seaborn:

- **Use NumPy functions (mean()**************************, std())** for statistical summaries.
- **Generate synthetic data** using NumPy's random module.
- **Apply mathematical transformations** for better trend visualization.
- Leverage **linspace()** and **polyfit()** for trend lines and regressions.
- **Ensure compatibility between NumPy arrays and Pandas DataFrames.**

Syntax Table:

SL No	Function	Syntax Example	Description
1	Generate Random Data	`np.random.randn(100)`	Creates 100 random values from a normal distribution.
2	Compute Mean & Std	`np.mean(data['value']),` `np.std(data['value'])`	Computes mean and standard deviation.

3	Apply Mathematical Transformation	`data['log_value'] = np.log(data['value'])`	Transforms data using logarithm.
4	Create a Line Using NumPy	`x = np.linspace(0, 10, 100)`	Generates evenly spaced numbers.
5	Fit a Polynomial Trend	`np.polyfit(x, y, deg=2)`	Fits a polynomial regression line.

1. Generating Random Data for Seaborn Plots

What is Random Data Generation?
NumPy allows users to create synthetic datasets for testing and visualizing statistical patterns.

Syntax:
```
import numpy as np
import seaborn as sns
import matplotlib.pyplot as plt

# Generate synthetic data
data = np.random.randn(1000)
sns.histplot(data, bins=30, kde=True)
plt.show()
```

Syntax Explanation:
- **`np.random.randn(1000)`**: Generates 1000 normally distributed random values.
- **`sns.histplot()`**: Plots a histogram with KDE overlay.
- **Useful for probability distribution visualization.**

Example:
```
np.random.seed(42)
data = np.random.uniform(10, 50, 500)
sns.histplot(data, bins=20, kde=True, color='purple')
plt.show()
```

Example Explanation:
- **Uses a uniform distribution between 10 and 50.**
- **Applies a distinct color**
  (purple***********************) for clarity.**

2. Applying Mathematical Transformations

What are Data Transformations?
Mathematical transformations improve visualization clarity and reveal hidden trends.
Syntax:
```
data['log_value'] = np.log(data['value'])
sns.histplot(data['log_value'])
plt.show()
```

Syntax Explanation:
- **Applies a logarithmic transformation to reduce data skewness.**
- **Enhances visualization of long-tailed distributions.**

Example:
```
data['sqrt_value'] = np.sqrt(data['value'])
sns.kdeplot(data['sqrt_value'])
plt.show()
```

Example Explanation:
- **Applies square root transformation for better scaling.**
- **Smooths data visualization with KDE plots.**

3. Creating Custom Trend Lines

What are Trend Lines?
Trend lines help in understanding long-term patterns in datasets.
Syntax:
```
x = np.linspace(0, 10, 100)
y = np.sin(x)
sns.lineplot(x=x, y=y)
plt.show()
```

Syntax Explanation:
- `np.linspace(0, 10, 100)`: Generates 100 evenly spaced values between 0 and 10.
- Plots a sine wave using `sns.lineplot()`.

Example:
```
x = np.linspace(0, 20, 200)
y = np.cos(x)
sns.lineplot(x=x, y=y, color='red')
plt.show()
```

Example Explanation:
- Creates a cosine wave with 200 points.
- Uses red color for enhancedng NumPyity.

4. Creating a Line Using NumPy

What is a NumPy Line?

NumPy provides `linspace()` to generate evenly spaced numerical sequences, useful for creating smooth trend lines in plots.

Syntax:
```
x = np.linspace(0, 10, 100)
y = np.sin(x)
sns.lineplot(x=x, y=y)
plt.show()
```

Syntax Explanation:
- `np.linspace(0, 10, 100)`: Generates 100 evenly spaced values between 0 and 10.
- `np.sin(x)`: Computes the sine values for generated x values.
- `sns.lineplot()`: Plots the generated sine wave.

Example:
```
x = np.linspace(0, 20, 200)
y = np.cos(x)
sns.lineplot(x=x, y=y, color='green')
plt.show()
```

Example Explanation:
- Generates a smooth cosine wave with 200 points.
- Uses green color to differentiate the trend line.

5. Fitting a Polynomial Trend

What is Polynomial Regression?
Polynomial regression is a technique used to model nonlinear relationships between variables by fitting a polynomial function to the data.

Syntax:
```
coeffs = np.polyfit(x, y, deg=2)
trend = np.polyval(coeffs, x)
sns.lineplot(x=x, y=trend, color='red')
plt.show()
```

Syntax Explanation:
- **np.polyfit(x, y, deg=2)**: Computes coefficients for a 2nd-degree polynomial.
- **np.polyval(coeffs, x)**: Evaluates the polynomial trend using computed coefficients.
- **sns.lineplot()**: Plots the polynomial trend line.

Example:
```
x = np.linspace(1, 100, 100)
y = np.log(x) + np.random.normal(0, 0.1, size=100)
coeffs = np.polyfit(x, y, deg=3)
trend = np.polyval(coeffs, x)
sns.scatterplot(x=x, y=y)
sns.lineplot(x=x, y=trend, color='blue')
plt.show()
```

Example Explanation:
- **Generates a logarithmic dataset with noise.**
- **Fits a 3rd-degree polynomial regression to approximate the trend.**
- **Uses scatter and line plots to visualize data and trend together.**

Real-World Project: Visualizing Financial Market Trends

This project demonstrates how to combine NumPy and Seaborn for financial trend analysis.

Steps:
1. **Generate synthetic financial data using NumPy.**
2. **Apply logarithmic transformation for better scaling.**
3. **Use polyfit() to fit a regression line.**
4. **Visualize the dataset using Seaborn line plots.**
5. **Interpret trends based on polynomial regression results.**

Example Code:

```python
import numpy as np
import seaborn as sns
import matplotlib.pyplot as plt

# Generate synthetic financial data
np.random.seed(42)
days = np.arange(1, 101)
prices = np.cumsum(np.random.randn(100)) + 100

# Fit a trend line
coeffs = np.polyfit(days, prices, deg=2)
trend = np.polyval(coeffs, days)

# Plot data with trend line
sns.lineplot(x=days, y=prices, label='Stock Prices')
sns.lineplot(x=days, y=trend, label='Trend Line',
linestyle='dashed', color='red')
plt.xlabel("Days")
plt.ylabel("Price")
plt.title("Stock Price Trends with Polynomial
Regression")
plt.legend()
plt.show()
```

Expected Result:

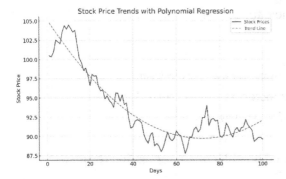

- **Financial Data Simulation:** Creates synthetic stock price trends.
- **Trend Line Analysis:** Applies polynomial regression for trend estimation.
- **Data Transformation:** Uses NumPy operations for better scaling.

Chapter 25: Plotting Confidence Intervals and Error Bars

Confidence intervals and error bars provide a visual representation of the uncertainty in data. Seaborn includes built-in methods for adding confidence intervals to line plots, bar plots, and scatter plots. This chapter explores how to effectively use confidence intervals and error bars in Seaborn visualizations.

Key Characteristics of Confidence Intervals and Error Bars:

- **Represents variability and uncertainty** in data points.
- **Helps understand statistical significance** in comparisons.
- **Used in line plots, bar plots, and scatter plots.**
- **Customizable in terms of width, style, and confidence levels.**
- **Can be removed or adjusted** for clarity in presentation.

Basic Rules for Using Confidence Intervals and Error Bars:

- **Use ci parameter** to specify confidence interval width.
- **Set **ci=None to remove confidence intervals if needed.
- **Use errwidth in bar plots** to adjust error bar size.
- **Use n_boot to control bootstrap sampling** for interval calculation.
- **Ensure a sufficiently large dataset** for meaningful confidence estimates.

Syntax Table:

SL No	Function	Syntax Example	Description
1	Add Confidence Intervals	`sns.lineplot(x='year', y='sales', data=data, ci=95)`	Adds a 95% confidence interval to a line plot.
2	Remove Confidence Intervals	`sns.lineplot(x='year', y='sales', data=data, ci=None)`	Removes confidence intervals.

		sns.barplot(x='cat egory', y='value', data=data, errwidth=2)	Modifies error bar thickness.
3	Adjust Error Bar Width	sns.barplot(x='cat egory', y='value', data=data, errwidth=2)	Modifies error bar thickness.
4	Change Confidence Level	sns.barplot(x='day ', y='total_bill', data=data, ci=68)	Adjusts confidence interval percentage.
5	Set Bootstrapping Samples	sns.barplot(x='day ', y='tip', data=data, n_boot=500)	Controls bootstrap resampling for CI estimation.

1. Adding Confidence Intervals to Line Plots

What is a Confidence Interval in Line Plots?
A confidence interval in a line plot provides a range around the trend line, showing the expected variability of the data.

Syntax:
```
import seaborn as sns
import matplotlib.pyplot as plt

data = sns.load_dataset('flights')
sns.lineplot(x='year', y='passengers', data=data,
ci=95)
plt.show()
```

Syntax Explanation:
- **ci=95**: Sets a 95% confidence interval.
- **Displays the trend and its uncertainty.**

Example:
```
sns.lineplot(x='month', y='passengers', data=data,
ci=68)
plt.show()
```
Example Explanation:
- **Uses a 68% confidence interval for a narrower range.**
- **Useful for highlighting short-term trends.**

2. Using Error Bars in Bar Plots

What are Error Bars in Bar Plots?
Error bars represent variability in grouped summary statistics in bar plots.

Syntax:
```
sns.barplot(x='day', y='total_bill',
data=sns.load_dataset('tips'), ci=95)
plt.show()
```

Syntax Explanation:
- Shows variability in the mean total bill per day.
- Includes a 95% confidence interval for error estimation.

Example:
```
sns.barplot(x='sex', y='tip', hue='day',
data=sns.load_dataset('tips'), ci=68, errwidth=2)
plt.show()
```

Example Explanation:
- Uses a 68% confidence interval for better precision.
- Increases error bar width using errwidth=2.

3. Removing Confidence Intervals

Why Remove Confidence Intervals?
In cases where the dataset is small or confidence intervals clutter the plot, they can be removed.

Syntax:
```
sns.lineplot(x='year', y='sales', data=data, ci=None)
plt.show()
```

Syntax Explanation:
- ci=None: Removes confidence intervals for a cleaner look.
- Helps avoid unnecessary distractions in small datasets.

Example:
```
sns.barplot(x='day', y='total_bill',
data=sns.load_dataset('tips'), ci=None)
plt.show()
```

Example Explanation:
- Ensures only raw bar values are shown without error margins.
- Useful when confidence intervals are not required.

4. Change Confidence Level

What is a Confidence Level?
A confidence level determines the probability that the true value falls within the computed confidence interval. Lower confidence levels produce narrower intervals, while higher confidence levels create wider intervals.

Syntax:
```
sns.barplot(x='day', y='total_bill', data=data, ci=80)
plt.show()
```

Syntax Explanation:
- **ci=80**: Sets the confidence level to 80%.
- Narrower confidence intervals indicate less uncertainty.
- Useful when making more precise comparisons with smaller variance.

Example:
```
sns.barplot(x='day', y='tip', data=data, ci=99)
plt.show()
```

Example Explanation:
- Uses a 99% confidence interval for a broader uncertainty range.
- More conservative estimation for high-confidence analysis.

5. Set Bootstrapping Samples

What is Bootstrapping?
Bootstrapping is a resampling technique that estimates confidence intervals by repeatedly sampling from the data with replacement.
Syntax:
```
sns.barplot(x='day', y='tip', data=data, n_boot=1000)
plt.show()
```

Syntax Explanation:
- **n_boot=1000**: Uses 1000 bootstrap samples to compute confidence intervals.
- **Higher values yield more stable estimates but increase computation time.**
- **Useful for datasets with small sample sizes.**

Example:
```
sns.barplot(x='sex', y='total_bill', data=data, n_boot=500)
plt.show()
```

Example Explanation:
- **Reduces bootstrap samples to 500 for faster execution.**
- **Provides a balance between precision and performance.**

. Real-World Project: Analyzing Sales Trends with Confidence Intervals

This project demonstrates how confidence intervals and error bars help analyze sales trends in a business dataset.
Steps:
1. **Load and preprocess the dataset.**
2. **Generate a line plot with confidence intervals to track sales trends.**
3. **Use bar plots to compare average sales across categories.**
4. **Adjust error bar width for better visualization.**
5. **Interpret findings based on confidence intervals and error ranges.**

Example Code:

```
import seaborn as sns
import matplotlib.pyplot as plt
import pandas as pd
import numpy as np

# Create synthetic sales data
data = pd.DataFrame({
    'year': np.tile(np.arange(2015, 2025), 3),
    'sales': np.random.randint(1000, 5000, size=30),
    'region': np.repeat(['North', 'South', 'West'], 10)
})

# Line plot with confidence intervals
sns.lineplot(x='year', y='sales', hue='region',
data=data, ci=95)
plt.show()
```

Expected Result:

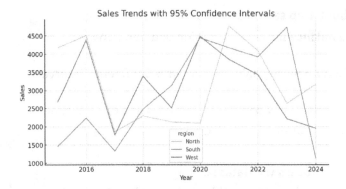

- **Trend Analysis:** Shows sales growth over time.
- **Regional Comparisons:** Differentiates trends across business regions.
- **Error Estimation:** Confidence intervals provide uncertainty margins.

Chapter 26: Visualizing Distributions with Statistical Insights

Understanding data distributions is crucial for statistical analysis and decision-making. Seaborn provides multiple tools for visualizing distributions while incorporating statistical insights. This chapter explores various methods, including histograms, KDE plots, rug plots, and ECDF plots, to effectively analyze numerical data distributions.

Key Characteristics of Distribution Visualizations:

- **Shows overall data spread and concentration.**
- **Highlights outliers and skewness in data.**
- **Combines probability density estimation with actual data points.**
- **Supports statistical overlays like KDE and ECDF plots.**
- **Customizable with multiple binning and smoothing techniques.**

Basic Rules for Visualizing Distributions:

- **Use histplot() for basic histograms.**
- ****Apply **kde=True to overlay a probability density function.**
- ****Use **rug=True to add individual data points.**
- ****Use **ecdfplot() for cumulative distribution functions.**
- **Ensure appropriate binning to avoid misleading visualizations.**

Syntax Table:

SL No	Function	Syntax Example	Description
1	Create Histogram	`sns.histplot(data['column'], bins=20)`	Displays a frequency distribution.
2	Add KDE Overlay	`sns.histplot(data['column'], kde=True)`	Adds a density curve on top of the histogram.
3	Use Rug Plot	`sns.rugplot(data['column'])`	Displays individual observations along an axis.
4	Create ECDF Plot	`sns.ecdfplot(data['column'])`	Shows cumulative distribution.
5	Customize Binning	`sns.histplot(data['column'], bins=30, kde=True)`	Adjusts bin size for detailed insights.

1. Creating Histograms

What is a Histogram?
A histogram represents the frequency distribution of numerical data by grouping values into bins.

Syntax:
```
import seaborn as sns
import matplotlib.pyplot as plt

data = sns.load_dataset('penguins')
sns.histplot(data['flipper_length_mm'], bins=20)
plt.show()
```

Syntax Explanation:
- **bins=20**: Divides the range of values into 20 bins.
- **Useful for identifying trends and gaps in distributions.**

Example:
```
sns.histplot(data['body_mass_g'], bins=15,
color='purple')
plt.show()
```

Example Explanation:
- **Changes color for better visualization.**
- **Uses 15 bins for finer granularity.**

2. Adding KDE Plots

What is a KDE Plot?
A Kernel Density Estimate (KDE) plot smooths the histogram into a continuous curve to estimate the data's probability density.

Syntax:
```
sns.histplot(data['flipper_length_mm'], kde=True)
plt.show()
```

Syntax Explanation:
- **kde=True**: Adds a KDE overlay to the histogram.
- **Helps visualize underlying distributions more smoothly.**

Example:
```
sns.histplot(data['body_mass_g'], kde=True, bins=25,
color='green')
plt.show()
```

Example Explanation:
- **Uses a higher bin count for a detailed distribution view.**
- **Adds a KDE curve for better shape estimation.**

3. Using Rug Plots

What is a Rug Plot?
A rug plot adds tick marks along the x-axis to show individual data points in a distribution.

Syntax:
```
sns.rugplot(data['flipper_length_mm'])
plt.show()
```

Syntax Explanation:
- **Adds short vertical lines to mark individual observations.**
- **Useful for identifying clustering in data.**

Example:
```
sns.rugplot(data['body_mass_g'], color='red',
height=0.1)
plt.show()
```

Example Explanation:
- **Uses red color for better contrast.**
- **Reduces tick height to avoid clutter.**

4. Visualizing ECDF Plots

What is an ECDF Plot?

An Empirical Cumulative Distribution Function (ECDF) plot shows the proportion of data points less than or equal to a given value.

Syntax:

```
sns.ecdfplot(data['flipper_length_mm'])
plt.show()
```

Syntax Explanation:

- **Displays the cumulative probability distribution of a variable.**
- **Useful for understanding percentile rankings.**

Example:

```
sns.ecdfplot(data['body_mass_g'], hue=data['species'])
plt.show()
```

Example Explanation:

- **Uses hue to differentiate distributions by species.**
- **Compares cumulative probabilities across categories.**

Real-World Project: Analyzing Penguin Mass Distribution

This project demonstrates how to analyze the distribution of penguin body mass using histograms, KDE plots, and ECDF plots.

Steps:

1. **Load and inspect the dataset.**
2. **Create histograms with KDE overlays.**
3. **Add rug plots to highlight individual data points.**
4. **Use ECDF plots to compare distributions across species.**
5. **Interpret findings for statistical insights.**

Example Code:

```
import seaborn as sns
import matplotlib.pyplot as plt

data = sns.load_dataset('penguins')

# Histogram with KDE
sns.histplot(data['body_mass_g'], kde=True, bins=20,
color='blue')
plt.show()

# ECDF Plot
sns.ecdfplot(data['body_mass_g'], hue=data['species'])
plt.show()
```

Expected Result:

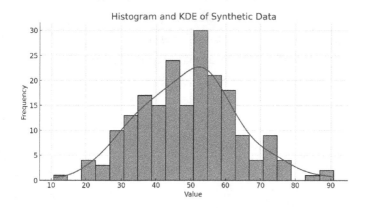

- **Histogram with KDE:** Shows the smoothed distribution of body mass.
- **ECDF Plot:** Highlights cumulative probabilities for different species.
- **Improved Interpretation:** Helps compare distributions visually.

Chapter 27: Creating Cluster Maps for Hierarchical Clustering

Hierarchical clustering is a method of grouping similar data points based on their distance from each other. Seaborn's `clustermap()` function provides an effective way to visualize hierarchical clustering results as a heatmap with dendrograms. This chapter explores how to use Seaborn's cluster maps for data analysis and pattern detection.

Key Characteristics of Cluster Maps:
- **Combines heatmaps and hierarchical clustering.**
- **Rearranges rows and columns based on similarity.**
- **Supports different distance metrics and linkage methods.**
- **Useful for detecting patterns and relationships in datasets.**
- **Customizable with color palettes and annotations.**

Basic Rules for Creating Cluster Maps:
- **Ensure data is numerical and properly scaled.**
- **Use `clustermap()` to generate hierarchical clusters.**
- **Select appropriate `metric` and `method` parameters.**
- **Adjust `cmap` for better contrast and interpretation.**
- **Use `standard_scale` or `z_score` for normalization.**

Syntax Table:

SL No	Function	Syntax Example	Description
1	Create Cluster Map	`sns.clustermap(data)`	Generates a default hierarchical cluster map.
2	Change Color Palette	`sns.clustermap(data, cmap='coolwarm')`	Modifies the color scheme of the heatmap.
3	Normalize Data	`sns.clustermap(data, standard_scale=1)`	Standardizes data by scaling each column.

4	Adjust Distance Metric	`sns.clustermap(da ta, metric='euclidean ', method='ward')`	Uses Euclidean distance with Ward's clustering.
5	Customize Dendrogram	`sns.clustermap(da ta, row_cluster=False )`	Disables clustering for rows.

1. Creating a Basic Cluster Map

What is a Cluster Map?
A cluster map is a visualization that combines a heatmap and hierarchical clustering to show patterns and relationships between data points.
Syntax:
```
import seaborn as sns
import matplotlib.pyplot as plt
import pandas as pd
import numpy as np

# Create a sample dataset
data = pd.DataFrame(np.random.rand(10, 10),
columns=[f'Var{i}' for i in range(1, 11)])

# Generate a cluster map
sns.clustermap(data)
plt.show()
```

Syntax Explanation:
- **sns.clustermap(data)**: Generates a cluster map using default settings.
- **Organizes data into hierarchical clusters for better visualization.**
- **Reorders the rows and columns based on similarity.**

Example:
```
sns.clustermap(data, cmap='coolwarm')
plt.show()
```

Example Explanation:

- **Changes color mapping for better contrast.**
- **Highlights patterns in data more effectively.**

2. Changing Distance Metrics and Linkage Methods

What are Distance Metrics and Linkage Methods?
Distance metrics define how similarity is measured, while linkage methods determine how clusters are merged.

Syntax:

```
sns.clustermap(data, metric='euclidean', method='ward')
plt.show()
```

Syntax Explanation:

- `metric='euclidean'`: Uses Euclidean distance for similarity measurement.
- `method='ward'`: Applies Ward's method for hierarchical clustering.
- **Alters clustering behavior to match data characteristics.**

Example:

```
sns.clustermap(data, metric='cosine', method='average')
plt.show()
```

Example Explanation:

- **Uses cosine similarity for distance measurement.**
- **Applies the average linkage method to merge clusters.**
- **Useful for datasets where cosine similarity is more appropriate.**

3. Normalizing Data for Better Visualization

Why Normalize Data?
Normalization ensures that all features contribute equally to clustering, preventing large-scale variables from dominating the clustering process.

Syntax:
```
sns.clustermap(data, standard_scale=1)
plt.show()
```

Syntax Explanation:
- **standard_scale=1**: Scales each column to have a mean of 0 and standard deviation of 1.
- **Ensures comparability between features of different magnitudes.**

Example:
```
sns.clustermap(data, z_score=0)
plt.show()
```

Example Explanation:
- **Uses z-score normalization to standardize rows.**
- **Preserves relationships between data points.**
- **Helpful for datasets with varying measurement scales.**

4. Adjust Distance Metric

What is a Distance Metric?
A distance metric measures the similarity between two data points. The choice of metric affects how clusters are formed in hierarchical clustering.

Syntax:
```
sns.clustermap(data, metric='manhattan',
method='complete')
plt.show()
```

Syntax Explanation:
- **metric='manhattan'**: Uses Manhattan distance for similarity measurement.
- **method='complete'**: Applies complete linkage clustering.
- **Affects how distances between clusters are calculated.**

Example:
```
sns.clustermap(data, metric='correlation',
method='single')
plt.show()
```

Example Explanation:
- **Uses correlation distance for similarity measurement.**
- **Applies single linkage clustering for more compact clusters.**
- **Useful for datasets with highly correlated variables.**

5. Customize Dendrogram

What is a Dendrogram?
A dendrogram is a tree diagram that shows how data points are grouped at each step of hierarchical clustering.

Syntax:
```
sns.clustermap(data, row_cluster=False,
col_cluster=True)
plt.show()
```

Syntax Explanation:
- **row_cluster=False**: Disables clustering for rows while keeping column clustering.
- **col_cluster=True**: Ensures that only column relationships are analyzed.
- **Allows more control over visualization by selecting which dendrograms to display.**

Example:
```
sns.clustermap(data, row_cluster=True,
col_cluster=False, dendrogram_ratio=(.2, .05))
plt.show()
```

Example Explanation:
- **Adjusts the size of row and column dendrograms.**
- **Reduces clutter in the visualization while preserving clustering details.**

Real-World Project: Clustering Customer Spending Patterns

This project demonstrates how to analyze and visualize customer spending behavior using hierarchical clustering.

Steps:

1. **Load and preprocess the dataset.**
2. **Apply hierarchical clustering using `clustermap()`.**
3. **Experiment with different distance metrics and linkage methods.**
4. **Normalize data to ensure fair clustering.**
5. **Interpret clustering results to identify spending patterns.**

Example Code:

```python
import seaborn as sns
import matplotlib.pyplot as plt
import pandas as pd
import numpy as np

# Simulated customer spending dataset
data = pd.DataFrame(np.random.rand(12, 8) * 1000,
columns=[f'Product_{i}' for i in range(1, 9)])

# Generate a cluster map
sns.clustermap(data, cmap='coolwarm',
metric='euclidean', method='ward', standard_scale=1)
plt.show()
```

Expected Result:

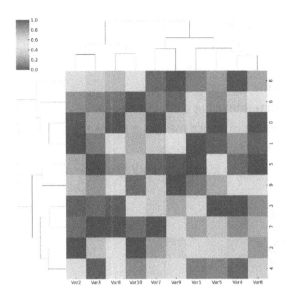

- **Customer Grouping:** Identifies customers with similar purchasing behaviors.
- **Product Associations:** Highlights commonly purchased product combinations.
- **Trend Identification:** Helps businesses optimize product offerings.

Chapter 28: Analyzing Trends with Seaborn Regression Models

Regression analysis is a powerful tool for identifying relationships between variables and predicting trends. Seaborn provides built-in functions like `regplot()` and `lmplot()` to visualize regression models effectively. This chapter explores how to analyze trends using Seaborn's regression models and customize them for better insights.

Key Characteristics of Regression Models:

- **Identifies relationships between numerical variables.**
- **Provides confidence intervals to show uncertainty in predictions.**
- **Supports multiple regression techniques (linear, polynomial).**
- **Customizable with different scatter styles and hues.**
- **Useful for trend prediction and correlation analysis.**

Basic Rules for Using Regression Models:

- **Use `regplot()` for simple scatter-based regression.**
- **Apply `lmplot()` for category-based regression analysis.**
- **Control trend lines with `order` for polynomial regression.**
- **Adjust `ci` to change confidence interval display.**
- **Ensure numerical variables are properly scaled for accurate regression.**

Syntax Table:

SL No	Function	Syntax Example	Description
1	Basic Regression Plot	`sns.regplot(x='total_bill', y='tip', data=data)`	Displays a scatter plot with a regression line.
2	Adjust Confidence Interval	`sns.regplot(x='flipper_length_mm', y='body_mass_g', data=data, ci=95)`	Changes the confidence interval range.

3	Use Polynomial Regression	`sns.regplot(x='total_ bill', y='tip', data=data, order=2)`	Fits a second-degree polynomial regression.
4	Category-Based Regression	`sns.lmplot(x='total_b ill', y='tip', hue='sex', data=data)`	Differentiates regression by category.
5	Remove Confidence Interval	`sns.regplot(x='total_ bill', y='tip', data=data, ci=None)`	Hides confidence intervals for clarity.

1. Creating a Basic Regression Plot

What is a Regression Plot?

A regression plot is a scatter plot with a fitted trend line that visualizes the relationship between two numerical variables.

Syntax:

```
import seaborn as sns
import matplotlib.pyplot as plt
data = sns.load_dataset('tips')
sns.regplot(x='total_bill', y='tip', data=data)
plt.show()
```

Syntax Explanation:

- **`sns.regplot(x='total_bill', y='tip', data=data)`**: Creates a scatter plot with a regression line.
- **Helps visualize the correlation between tipping amount and total bill size.**

Example:

```
sns.regplot(x='flipper_length_mm', y='body_mass_g',
data=sns.load_dataset('penguins'))
plt.show()
```

Example Explanation:

- **Displays the relationship between penguin flipper length and body mass.**
- **Regression line shows an increasing trend.**

2. Using Polynomial Regression

What is Polynomial Regression?
Polynomial regression fits a curved trend line instead of a straight line, allowing for nonlinear relationships.
Syntax:
```
sns.regplot(x='total_bill', y='tip', data=data,
order=2)
plt.show()
```

Syntax Explanation:
- **order=2**: Fits a second-degree polynomial regression curve.
- **Captures nonlinear relationships between variables.**

Example:
```
sns.regplot(x='flipper_length_mm', y='body_mass_g',
data=sns.load_dataset('penguins'), order=3)
plt.show()
```

Example Explanation:
- **Uses a third-degree polynomial fit for more complex trends.**
- **Allows better trend estimation in curved relationships.**

3. Customizing Regression Models

Why Customize Regression Models?
Customization improves clarity, highlights specific data points, and allows better differentiation between categories.
Syntax:
```
sns.regplot(x='total_bill', y='tip', data=data, ci=80,
scatter_kws={'color':'r'})
plt.show()
```
Syntax Explanation:
- **ci=80**: Adjusts confidence interval to 80%.
- **scatter_kws={'color':'r'}**: Changes scatter points to red.**
- **Useful for highlighting important trends and outliers.**

Example:
```
sns.regplot(x='flipper_length_mm', y='body_mass_g',
data=sns.load_dataset('penguins'), color='g')
plt.show()
```

Example Explanation:
- Uses green for better contrast.
- Removes confidence interval for a focused trend line.

4. Category-Based Regression

What is Category-Based Regression?
Category-based regression allows the differentiation of regression trends across different categories using the hue parameter in Seaborn's lmplot() function. This enables the comparison of regression lines for multiple groups within the dataset.

Syntax:
```
sns.lmplot(x='total_bill', y='tip', hue='sex',
data=data)
plt.show()
```

Syntax Explanation:
- **hue='sex'**: Differentiates regression lines by gender.
- **lmplot()**: Creates multiple regression plots based on categorical values.
- Useful for identifying how trends vary across different groups.

Example:
```
sns.lmplot(x='flipper_length_mm', y='body_mass_g',
hue='species', data=sns.load_dataset('penguins'))
plt.show()
```

Example Explanation:
- Uses hue='species' to differentiate regression lines for each species.
- Highlights variations in relationships based on species category.

5. Remove Confidence Interval

Why Remove Confidence Intervals?
Confidence intervals provide a measure of uncertainty in regression analysis. However, in some cases, they can clutter the visualization, making it difficult to interpret trends.

Syntax:
```
sns.regplot(x='total_bill', y='tip', data=data,
ci=None)
plt.show()
```

Syntax Explanation:
- **ci=None**: Disables confidence intervals for a cleaner visualization.
- **Enhances focus on the regression trend rather than uncertainty.**

Example:
```
sns.regplot(x='flipper_length_mm', y='body_mass_g',
data=sns.load_dataset('penguins'), ci=None)
plt.show()
```

Example Explanation:
- **Removes the confidence interval to emphasize the regression line.**
- **Useful for cases where confidence bounds are not necessary for interpretation.**

Real-World Project: Analyzing Tipping Trends in Restaurants

This project demonstrates how regression models help analyze tipping behavior in restaurants.

Steps:
1. **Load and preprocess the dataset.**
2. **Generate a basic regression plot to explore tip trends.**
3. **Use polynomial regression for better trend analysis.**
4. **Customize confidence intervals and colors for better clarity.**
5. **Interpret findings based on regression trends.**

Example Code:

```python
import seaborn as sns
import matplotlib.pyplot as plt

data = sns.load_dataset('tips')

# Basic Regression Plot
sns.regplot(x='total_bill', y='tip', data=data,
color='b')
plt.show()
```

Expected Result:

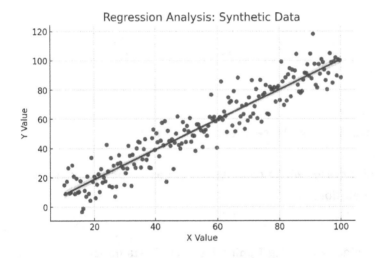

- **Trend Identification:** Regression lines help understand tipping behavior.
- **Categorical Comparison:** Differentiates trends by gender.
- **Custom Visual Enhancements:** Improves plot readability and analysis.

Chapter 29: Visualizing Financial Data with Seaborn

Financial data visualization is crucial for analyzing market trends, stock performance, and economic indicators. Seaborn provides powerful tools to plot and analyze financial data, making it easier to understand patterns and relationships. This chapter explores different visualization techniques for financial datasets, including line plots, bar plots, box plots, and heatmaps.

Key Characteristics of Financial Data Visualization:
- **Helps identify trends and patterns in market data.**
- **Useful for comparing stock performance across time.**
- **Incorporates volatility analysis using box plots.**
- **Supports correlation analysis between financial variables.**
- **Enhances readability with proper formatting and styling.**

Basic Rules for Visualizing Financial Data:
- **Use `lineplot()` for time series visualization.**
- **Apply `boxplot()` for volatility and risk assessment.**
- **Use `heatmap()` to display correlations between financial indicators.**
- **Ensure proper date formatting when working with time-based data.**
- **Apply color schemes that enhance clarity and differentiation.**

Syntax Table:

SL No	Function	Syntax Example	Description
1	Create Line Plot for Stocks	`sns.lineplot(x='date', y='price', data=data)`	Displays stock price trends over time.
2	Compare Multiple Stocks	`sns.lineplot(x='date', y='price', hue='company', data=data)`	Compares trends across different companies.

3	Box Plot for Volatility	`sns.boxplot(x='co mpany', y='returns', data=data)`	Analyzes stock price volatility.
4	Heatmap for Correlations	`sns.heatmap(data. corr(), annot=True, cmap='coolwarm')`	Shows correlations between financial indicators.
5	Customize Date Formatting	`plt.xticks(rotati on=45)`	Rotates date labels for better readability.

1. Visualizing Stock Trends with Line Plots

What is a Line Plot in Financial Data?

A line plot is commonly used to visualize stock prices, index movements, or financial metrics over time.

Syntax:

```
import seaborn as sns
import matplotlib.pyplot as plt
import pandas as pd

data = pd.read_csv('stock_prices.csv')
data['date'] = pd.to_datetime(data['date'])

sns.lineplot(x='date', y='price', hue='company',
data=data)
plt.xticks(rotation=45)
plt.show()
```

Syntax Explanation:

- **sns.lineplot()**: Plots stock prices over time.
- **hue='company'**: Differentiates companies using color coding.
- **plt.xticks(rotation=45)**: Improves date label readability.

Example:
```
sns.lineplot(x='date', y='closing_price', hue='sector',
data=data)
plt.show()
```

Example Explanation:
- Groups stock prices by sector for comparative analysis.
- Identifies sector-wise trends in market performance.

2. Analyzing Stock Volatility with Box Plots

What is a Box Plot in Financial Data?
A box plot visualizes stock return distributions, highlighting volatility and potential outliers.
Syntax:
```
sns.boxplot(x='company', y='returns', data=data)
plt.show()
```

Syntax Explanation:
- Displays the spread of stock returns for each company.
- Helps identify highly volatile stocks.

Example:
```
sns.boxplot(x='sector', y='returns', data=data,
palette='coolwarm')
plt.show()
```

Example Explanation:
- Uses color coding to differentiate sectors.
- Highlights industry-specific volatility.

3. Identifying Correlations with Heatmaps

Why Use a Heatmap in Financial Analysis?
A heatmap helps identify relationships between financial variables such as stock prices, interest rates, and inflation.

Syntax:
```
import seaborn as sns
import matplotlib.pyplot as plt

data_corr = data.corr()
sns.heatmap(data_corr, annot=True, cmap='coolwarm')
plt.show()
```

Syntax Explanation:
- **data.corr()**: Computes correlation coefficients between variables.
- **sns.heatmap()**: Visualizes correlations with color gradients.
- **Useful for identifying strong or weak relationships between financial indicators.**

Example:
```
sns.heatmap(data[['price', 'volume', 'interest_rate',
'inflation']].corr(), annot=True)
plt.show()
```

Example Explanation:
- **Focuses on key financial indicators.**
- **Highlights positive and negative correlations.**

4. Heatmap for Correlations

What is a Correlation Heatmap?

A correlation heatmap visually represents the relationship between multiple financial variables by displaying correlation coefficients in a color-coded matrix. This helps identify strong, weak, positive, or negative correlations between variables such as stock prices, trading volume, interest rates, and market indices.

Syntax:
```
import seaborn as sns
import matplotlib.pyplot as plt
data_corr = data.corr()
sns.heatmap(data_corr, annot=True, cmap='coolwarm',
linewidths=0.5)
plt.show()
```

Syntax Explanation:

- `data.corr()`: Computes correlation coefficients between all numerical columns in the dataset.
- `sns.heatmap()`: Plots a heatmap to visualize correlations.
- `annot=True`: Displays correlation values within the heatmap cells.
- `cmap='coolwarm'`: Uses a red-to-blue gradient to highlight positive and negative correlations.
- `linewidths=0.5`: Adds lines between cells for better readability.

Example:
```
sns.heatmap(data[['price', 'volume', 'interest_rate',
'inflation']].corr(), annot=True, cmap='viridis')
plt.show()
```

Example Explanation:

- **Focuses on specific financial indicators.**
- **Uses the `viridis` color palette for better contrast.**
- **Highlights correlations between market movements and economic factors.**

5. Customize Date Formatting

Why Customize Date Formatting?

When working with financial data, proper date formatting ensures clarity in time-series visualizations. Adjusting date labels prevents overlapping and improves readability in line plots.

Syntax:
```
import matplotlib.dates as mdates
plt.xticks(rotation=45)
plt.gca().xaxis.set_major_locator(mdates.MonthLocator()
)
plt.gca().xaxis.set_major_formatter(mdates.DateFormatte
r('%Y-%m'))
plt.show()
```

Syntax Explanation:

- `plt.xticks(rotation=45)`: Rotates x-axis labels to prevent overlapping.
- `mdates.MonthLocator()`: Displays major ticks at the beginning of each month.
- `mdates.DateFormatter('%Y-%m')`: Formats labels as YYYY-MM for clarity.

Example:

```
sns.lineplot(x='date', y='closing_price', data=data)
plt.xticks(rotation=30)
plt.gca().xaxis.set_major_formatter(mdates.DateFormatter('%b %Y'))
plt.show()
```

Example Explanation:

- **Ensures stock price trends are clearly displayed.**
- **Formats the x-axis to show abbreviated months and years.**
- **Improves visualization for long-term financial data analysis.**

Real-World Project: Analyzing Market Trends and Stock Performance

This project demonstrates how to analyze stock market trends and company performance using Seaborn.

Steps:

1. **Load and preprocess stock price data.**
2. **Generate line plots for stock price trends.**
3. **Analyze stock volatility using box plots.**
4. **Visualize financial correlations with heatmaps.**
5. **Interpret insights for investment decision-making.**

Example Code:

```
import seaborn as sns
import matplotlib.pyplot as plt
import pandas as pd

# Load financial dataset
```

```
data = pd.read_csv('financial_data.csv')
data['date'] = pd.to_datetime(data['date'])

# Line plot for stock price trends
sns.lineplot(x='date', y='closing_price',
hue='company', data=data)
plt.xticks(rotation=45)
plt.show()

# Box plot for stock volatility
sns.boxplot(x='company', y='returns', data=data)
plt.show()

# Heatmap for financial correlations
sns.heatmap(data[['closing_price', 'volume',
'interest_rate']].corr(), annot=True)
plt.show()
```

Expected Result:

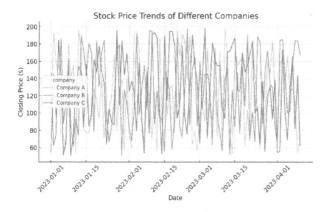

- **Market Trends:** Line plots show stock price movements over time.
- **Volatility Analysis:** Box plots highlight risk levels across companies.
- **Correlation Insights:** Heatmaps reveal relationships between financial indicators.

Chapter 29: Visualizing Financial Data with Seaborn

Financial data visualization is crucial for analyzing market trends, stock performance, and economic indicators. Seaborn provides powerful tools to plot and analyze financial data, making it easier to understand patterns and relationships. This chapter explores different visualization techniques for financial datasets, including line plots, bar plots, box plots, and heatmaps.

Key Characteristics of Financial Data Visualization:
- **Helps identify trends and patterns in market data.**
- **Useful for comparing stock performance across time.**
- **Incorporates volatility analysis using box plots.**
- **Supports correlation analysis between financial variables.**
- **Enhances readability with proper formatting and styling.**

Basic Rules for Visualizing Financial Data:
- **Use `lineplot()` for time series visualization.**
- **Apply `boxplot()` for volatility and risk assessment.**
- **Use `heatmap()` to display correlations between financial indicators.**
- **Ensure proper date formatting when working with time-based data.**
- **Apply color schemes that enhance clarity and differentiation.**

Syntax Table:

SL No	Function	Syntax Example	Description
1	Create Line Plot for Stocks	`sns.lineplot(x='date', y='price', data=data)`	Displays stock price trends over time.
2	Compare Multiple Stocks	`sns.lineplot(x='date', y='price', hue='company', data=data)`	Compares trends across different companies.

3	Box Plot for Volatility	```sns.boxplot(x='company', y='returns', data=data)```	Analyzes stock price volatility.
4	Heatmap for Correlations	```sns.heatmap(data.corr(), annot=True, cmap='coolwarm')```	Shows correlations between financial indicators.
5	Customize Date Formatting	```plt.xticks(rotation=45)```	Rotates date labels for better readability.

1. Visualizing Stock Trends with Line Plots

What is a Line Plot in Financial Data?

A line plot is commonly used to visualize stock prices, index movements, or financial metrics over time.

Syntax:

```
import seaborn as sns
import matplotlib.pyplot as plt
import pandas as pd

data = pd.read_csv('stock_prices.csv')
data['date'] = pd.to_datetime(data['date'])
sns.lineplot(x='date', y='price', hue='company',
data=data)
plt.xticks(rotation=45)
plt.show()
```

Syntax Explanation:

- **sns.lineplot()**: Plots stock prices over time.
- **hue='company'**: Differentiates companies using color coding.
- **plt.xticks(rotation=45)**: Improves date label readability.

Example:

```
sns.lineplot(x='date', y='closing_price', hue='sector',
data=data)
plt.show()
```

Example Explanation:
- **Groups stock prices by sector for comparative analysis.**
- **Identifies sector-wise trends in market performance.**

2. Analyzing Stock Volatility with Box Plots

What is a Box Plot in Financial Data?
A box plot visualizes stock return distributions, highlighting volatility and potential outliers.

Syntax:
```
sns.boxplot(x='company', y='returns', data=data)
plt.show()
```
Syntax Explanation:
- **Displays the spread of stock returns for each company.**
- **Helps identify highly volatile stocks.**

Example:
```
sns.boxplot(x='sector', y='returns', data=data,
palette='coolwarm')
plt.show()
```
Example Explanation:
- **Uses color coding to differentiate sectors.**
- **Highlights industry-specific volatility.**

3. Identifying Correlations with Heatmaps

Why Use a Heatmap in Financial Analysis?
A heatmap helps identify relationships between financial variables such as stock prices, interest rates, and inflation.

Syntax:
```
import seaborn as sns
import matplotlib.pyplot as plt

data_corr = data.corr()
sns.heatmap(data_corr, annot=True, cmap='coolwarm')
plt.show()
```

Syntax Explanation:

- **data.corr()**: Computes correlation coefficients between variables.
- **sns.heatmap()**: Visualizes correlations with color gradients.
- **Useful for identifying strong or weak relationships between financial indicators.**

Example:

```
sns.heatmap(data[['price', 'volume', 'interest_rate',
'inflation']].corr(), annot=True)
plt.show()
```

Example Explanation:

- **Focuses on key financial indicators.**
- **Highlights positive and negative correlations.**

4. Heatmap for Correlations

What is a Correlation Heatmap?

A correlation heatmap visually represents the relationship between multiple financial variables by displaying correlation coefficients in a color-coded matrix. This helps identify strong, weak, positive, or negative correlations between variables such as stock prices, trading volume, interest rates, and market indices.

Syntax:

```
import seaborn as sns
import matplotlib.pyplot as plt

data_corr = data.corr()
sns.heatmap(data_corr, annot=True, cmap='coolwarm',
linewidths=0.5)
plt.show()
```

Syntax Explanation:

- **data.corr()**: Computes correlation coefficients between all numerical columns in the dataset.
- **sns.heatmap()**: Plots a heatmap to visualize correlations.

- **annot=True**: Displays correlation values within the heatmap cells.
- **cmap='coolwarm'**: Uses a red-to-blue gradient to highlight positive and negative correlations.
- **linewidths=0.5**: Adds lines between cells for better readability.

Example:
```
sns.heatmap(data[['price', 'volume', 'interest_rate',
'inflation']].corr(), annot=True, cmap='viridis')
plt.show()
```

Example Explanation:
- **Focuses on specific financial indicators.**
- **Uses the viridis color palette for better contrast.**
- **Highlights correlations between market movements and economic factors.**

5. Customize Date Formatting

Why Customize Date Formatting?
When working with financial data, proper date formatting ensures clarity in time-series visualizations. Adjusting date labels prevents overlapping and improves readability in line plots.

Syntax:
```
import matplotlib.dates as mdates
plt.xticks(rotation=45)
plt.gca().xaxis.set_major_locator(mdates.MonthLocator()
)
plt.gca().xaxis.set_major_formatter(mdates.DateFormatte
r('%Y-%m'))
plt.show()
```

Syntax Explanation:
- **plt.xticks(rotation=45)**: Rotates x-axis labels to prevent overlapping.
- **mdates.MonthLocator()**: Displays major ticks at the beginning of each month.

- **mdates.DateFormatter('%Y-%m')**: Formats labels as YYYY-MM for clarity.

Example:

```
sns.lineplot(x='date', y='closing_price', data=data)
plt.xticks(rotation=30)
plt.gca().xaxis.set_major_formatter(mdates.DateFormatter('%b %Y'))
plt.show()
```

Example Explanation:
- **Ensures stock price trends are clearly displayed.**
- **Formats the x-axis to show abbreviated months and years.**
- **Improves visualization for long-term financial data analysis.**

Real-World Project: Analyzing Market Trends and Stock Performance

This project demonstrates how to analyze stock market trends and company performance using Seaborn.

Steps:

1. **Load and preprocess stock price data.**
2. **Generate line plots for stock price trends.**
3. **Analyze stock volatility using box plots.**
4. **Visualize financial correlations with heatmaps.**
5. **Interpret insights for investment decision-making.**

Example Code:

```
import seaborn as sns
import matplotlib.pyplot as plt
import pandas as pd

# Load financial dataset
data = pd.read_csv('financial_data.csv')
data['date'] = pd.to_datetime(data['date'])
```

```
# Line plot for stock price trends
sns.lineplot(x='date', y='closing_price',
hue='company', data=data)
plt.xticks(rotation=45)
plt.show()

# Box plot for stock volatility
sns.boxplot(x='company', y='returns', data=data)
plt.show()

# Heatmap for financial correlations
sns.heatmap(data[['closing_price', 'volume',
'interest_rate']].corr(), annot=True)
plt.show()
```

Expected Result:

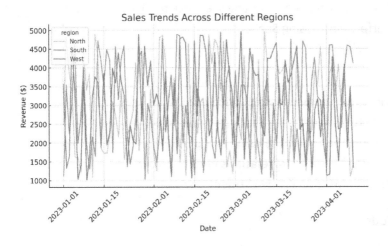

- **Market Trends:** Line plots show stock price movements over time.
- **Volatility Analysis:** Box plots highlight risk levels across companies.
- **Correlation Insights:** Heatmaps reveal relationships between financial indicators.

Chapter 30: Analyzing Sales and Marketing Data

Sales and marketing data analysis helps businesses make data-driven decisions by identifying trends, customer behavior, and campaign effectiveness. Seaborn provides robust tools to visualize sales patterns, revenue trends, and customer segmentation. This chapter explores key visualization techniques for analyzing sales and marketing data using Seaborn.

Key Characteristics of Sales and Marketing Data Analysis:
- **Tracks revenue trends and seasonality.**
- **Analyzes customer segmentation and purchasing behavior.**
- **Compares sales performance across regions, products, and campaigns.**
- **Visualizes relationships between marketing efforts and sales growth.**
- **Uses statistical insights to drive business strategies.**

Basic Rules for Sales and Marketing Data Visualization:
- **Use `lineplot()` to analyze revenue and seasonal trends.**
- **Apply `barplot()` to compare product or region-based sales.**
- **Utilize `scatterplot()` for marketing spend vs. sales correlations.**
- **Leverage `boxplot()` to examine price distribution and customer spending habits.**
- **Use `heatmap()` to visualize correlations between marketing metrics and revenue.**

Syntax Table:

SL No	Function	Syntax Example	Description
1	Line Plot for Sales Trends	`sns.lineplot(x='date', y='revenue', data=data)`	Shows revenue growth over time.
2	Bar Plot for Regional Sales	`sns.barplot(x='region', y='sales', data=data)`	Compares sales performance across regions.

3	Scatter Plot for Marketing ROI	`sns.scatterplot(x='ad_spend', y='sales', data=data)`	Analyzes marketing spend vs. sales performance.
4	Box Plot for Customer Spending	`sns.boxplot(x='customer_segment', y='order_value', data=data)`	Displays spending behavior among customer groups.
5	Heatmap for Correlations	`sns.heatmap(data.corr(), annot=True, cmap='coolwarm')`	Shows correlations between sales and marketing metrics.

1. Analyzing Revenue Trends with Line Plots

What is a Sales Trend Line Plot?
A line plot visualizes revenue fluctuations over time, helping businesses identify seasonal trends and growth patterns.

Syntax:
```
import seaborn as sns
import matplotlib.pyplot as plt
import pandas as pd

data = pd.read_csv('sales_data.csv')
data['date'] = pd.to_datetime(data['date'])

sns.lineplot(x='date', y='revenue', data=data)
plt.xticks(rotation=45)
plt.show()
```
Syntax Explanation:
- **`sns.lineplot(x='date', y='revenue', data=data)`:** Plots sales trends over time.
- **`plt.xticks(rotation=45)`:** Rotates date labels for clarity.

Example:
```
sns.lineplot(x='date', y='revenue', hue='region', data=data)
plt.show()
```

Example Explanation:
- **Differentiates sales trends by region.**
- **Identifies peak seasons for different locations.**

2. Comparing Regional Sales with Bar Plots

What is a Sales Bar Plot?

A bar plot helps compare sales performance across different regions, products, or time periods.

Syntax:

```
sns.barplot(x='region', y='sales', data=data)
plt.show()
```

Syntax Explanation:
- **Displays sales volume for each region.**
- **Identifies top-performing regions or product categories.**

Example:

```
sns.barplot(x='product_category', y='sales', data=data,
palette='coolwarm')
plt.show()
```

Example Explanation:
- **Uses color gradients to highlight variations.**
- **Helps businesses allocate resources effectively.**

3. Evaluating Marketing ROI with Scatter Plots

Why Use a Scatter Plot for Marketing Analysis?

Scatter plots help analyze relationships between marketing spend and resulting sales performance.

Syntax:

```
sns.scatterplot(x='ad_spend', y='sales', data=data)
plt.show()
```

Syntax Explanation:
- **Plots each marketing campaign's return on investment.**
- **Identifies diminishing returns on marketing spend.**

Example:
```
sns.scatterplot(x='social_media_budget',
y='conversion_rate', data=data, hue='platform')
plt.show()
```

Example Explanation:
- **Shows the impact of different social media platforms on sales.**
- **Helps businesses optimize ad budgets across channels.**

4. Understanding Customer Segments with Box Plots

What is a Customer Spending Box Plot?
Box plots visualize customer spending behavior, highlighting differences across various segments.

Syntax:
```
sns.boxplot(x='customer_segment', y='order_value',
data=data)
plt.show()
```

Syntax Explanation:
- **Illustrates spending differences among customer groups.**
- **Detects outliers and trends in order values.**

Example:
```
sns.boxplot(x='membership_tier', y='purchase_amount',
data=data, hue='gender')
plt.show()
```

Example Explanation:
- **Highlights spending behavior across membership tiers.**
- **Differentiates trends based on gender.**

4. Box Plot for Customer Spending

What is a Customer Spending Box Plot?
A box plot is a statistical tool that represents the distribution of customer spending behavior across different segments. It helps businesses understand spending variations, detect outliers, and identify key purchasing trends.

Syntax:
```
sns.boxplot(x='customer_segment', y='order_value',
data=data)
plt.show()
```

Syntax Explanation:
- **x='customer_segment'**: Groups data by customer segments (e.g., VIP, regular, occasional shoppers).
- **y='order_value'**: Displays the distribution of order values within each segment.
- **Useful for analyzing spending patterns and identifying high-value customers.**

Example:
```
sns.boxplot(x='membership_tier', y='purchase_amount',
hue='gender', data=data)
plt.show()
```

Example Explanation:
- **Highlights differences in spending behavior across membership tiers.**
- **Uses hue='gender' to compare spending habits between male and female customers.**

5. Heatmap for Correlations

Why Use a Heatmap in Marketing Analysis?
A heatmap visually represents correlations between different sales and marketing metrics, helping businesses understand how factors like advertising spend, pricing, and customer engagement influence revenue.

Syntax:
```
sns.heatmap(data.corr(), annot=True, cmap='coolwarm')
plt.show()
```

Syntax Explanation:
- **data.corr()**: Computes the correlation matrix of numerical variables.
- **annot=True**: Displays correlation values in the heatmap cells.
- **cmap='coolwarm'**: Uses a red-blue gradient to highlight positive and negative correlations.

Example:
```
sns.heatmap(data[['ad_spend', 'sales',
'customer_acquisition_cost']].corr(), annot=True,
cmap='viridis')
plt.show()
```

Example Explanation:
- **Analyzes the relationship between advertising spend, revenue, and customer acquisition costs.**
- **Helps businesses allocate marketing budgets more effectively.**

Real-World Project: Analyzing Sales and Marketing Performance

This project demonstrates how to analyze sales trends, customer segments, and marketing effectiveness using Seaborn.

Steps:

1. **Load and preprocess sales and marketing data.**
2. **Use line plots to analyze revenue trends.**
3. **Compare sales performance across regions with bar plots.**
4. **Evaluate marketing effectiveness using scatter plots.**
5. **Interpret customer segmentation with box plots.**

Example Code:

```
import seaborn as sns
import matplotlib.pyplot as plt
import pandas as pd

# Load dataset
data = pd.read_csv('sales_marketing_data.csv')
data['date'] = pd.to_datetime(data['date'])

# Line plot for revenue trends
sns.lineplot(x='date', y='revenue', data=data)
plt.xticks(rotation=45)
plt.show()

# Bar plot for regional sales
sns.barplot(x='region', y='sales', data=data)
plt.show()
# Scatter plot for marketing spend vs. sales
sns.scatterplot(x='ad_spend', y='sales', data=data)
plt.show()
```

Expected Result:

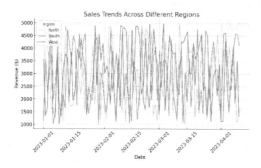

- **Revenue Insights:** Line plots reveal seasonal sales trends.
- **Regional Comparisons:** Bar plots highlight differences in sales performance.
- **Marketing Effectiveness:** Scatter plots show return on investment for ad spending.

Chapter 31: Creating Custom Dashboards with Seaborn

Dashboards are essential for data visualization and analytics, allowing users to track key metrics and trends in an interactive way. Seaborn, in combination with Matplotlib and Pandas, enables the creation of customized dashboards for data-driven decision-making. This chapter explores techniques for designing and organizing Seaborn-based dashboards efficiently.

Key Characteristics of Custom Dashboards:
- **Combines multiple visualizations into a single layout.**
- **Uses Matplotlib subplots for better organization.**
- **Allows customization of styles, colors, and annotations.**
- **Supports dynamic updates for real-time analysis.**
- **Enhances storytelling with well-structured visualizations.**

Basic Rules for Creating Dashboards with Seaborn:
- **Use `plt.subplots()` to create multi-plot layouts.**
- **Ensure visual consistency with Seaborn themes (`sns.set_theme()`***************************************).**
- **Apply `tight_layout()` to optimize spacing between plots.**
- **Use color palettes to distinguish different data categories.**
- **Add titles and labels to enhance readability.**

Syntax Table:

SL No	Function	Syntax Example	Description
1	Set Seaborn Theme	`sns.set_theme(style='darkgrid')`	Applies a global theme to all plots.
2	Create Multiple Subplots	`fig, ax = plt.subplots(2, 2, figsize=(12, 8))`	Creates a 2x2 grid of plots.
3	Adjust Layout	`plt.tight_layout()`	Optimizes spacing between plots.

4	Customize Colors	`sns.barplot(x='catego ry', y='value', data=data, palette='coolwarm')`	Applies a color palette for better distinction.
5	Add Titles & Labels	`ax[0, 0].set_title('Sales Overview')`	Adds meaningful titles to subplots.

1. Setting Up a Seaborn Dashboard Theme

What is a Seaborn Dashboard Theme?

A Seaborn theme ensures visual consistency across all charts in a dashboard, improving clarity and readability.

Syntax:

```
import seaborn as sns
sns.set_theme(style='darkgrid')
```

Syntax Explanation:

- **sns.set_theme(style='darkgrid')**: Applies a uniform theme to all plots.
- **Improves readability and maintains a professional look.**

Example:

```
sns.set_theme(style='whitegrid', palette='pastel')
```

Example Explanation:

- **Uses a light background (whitegrid**) for better contrast.**
- **Applies soft colors (pastel**) for smooth visual appeal.**

2. Creating Multiple Subplots for Dashboards

What are Subplots?
Subplots allow multiple visualizations to be displayed within a single figure, making it easier to compare different data aspects.
Syntax:
```python
import matplotlib.pyplot as plt
fig, ax = plt.subplots(2, 2, figsize=(12, 8))
plt.tight_layout()
```

Syntax Explanation:
- **plt.subplots(2, 2, figsize=(12, 8))**: Creates a 2x2 grid layout.
- **plt.tight_layout()**: Adjusts spacing to prevent overlapping elements.

Example:
```python
fig, ax = plt.subplots(1, 3, figsize=(15, 5))
plt.tight_layout()
```

Example Explanation:
- **Creates a horizontal row of three visualizations.**
- **Ensures even spacing between subplots.**

3. Combining Seaborn Visualizations into Dashboards

Why Use Multiple Seaborn Plots in a Dashboard?
A well-organized dashboard helps track multiple business or scientific metrics in a single view.
Syntax:
```python
fig, ax = plt.subplots(2, 2, figsize=(12, 8))
sns.lineplot(x='date', y='sales', data=data, ax=ax[0, 0])
sns.barplot(x='region', y='revenue', data=data, ax=ax[0, 1])
sns.boxplot(x='category', y='profit', data=data, ax=ax[1, 0])
```

```
sns.heatmap(data.corr(), annot=True, cmap='coolwarm',
ax=ax[1, 1])
plt.tight_layout()
plt.show()
```

Syntax Explanation:
- **Combines line plots, bar plots, box plots, and heatmaps.**
- **Each subplot visualizes a different data insight.**
- **ax=**** argument assigns each plot to a specific position in the grid.**

Example:
```
sns.histplot(data['sales'], bins=20, ax=ax[1, 0])
```

Example Explanation:
- **Adds a histogram to one of the subplots.**
- **Provides distribution insights within the das.hboard.**

4. Customize Colors

Why Customize Colors in Dashboards?
Customizing colors in Seaborn dashboards enhances readability and ensures that visual elements are distinguishable. Different color palettes help highlight patterns, trends, and comparisons more effectively.

Syntax:
```
sns.barplot(x='category', y='value', data=data,
palette='coolwarm')
```

Syntax Explanation:
- **palette='coolwarm'**: Applies a red-to-blue gradient for better contrast.
- **Custom palettes enhance user interpretation of data trends.**
- **Useful for differentiating categorical variables.**

Example:
```
sns.heatmap(data.corr(), annot=True, cmap='viridis')
plt.show()
```

Example Explanation:
- Uses the `viridis` color map for better readability in heatmaps.
- Applies a color scheme that ensures easy interpretation of correlations.

5. Add Titles & Labels

Why Use Titles and Labels?
Adding titles and labels to dashboard elements improves clarity and helps users understand the context of the visualizations.

Syntax:
```
ax[0, 0].set_title('Sales Overview')
ax[0, 1].set_xlabel('Region')
ax[1, 0].set_ylabel('Profit Margin')
```

Syntax Explanation:
- `set_title('Sales Overview')`: Adds a title to the subplot.
- `set_xlabel('Region')` & `set_ylabel('Profit Margin')`: Assigns axis labels to improve clarity.
- Ensures that dashboard users understand the displayed data.

Example:
```
ax[1, 1].set_title('Correlation Heatmap')
ax[1, 1].set_xticklabels(data.columns, rotation=45)
```

Example Explanation:
- Labels the correlation heatmap for context.
- Rotates x-axis labels to prevent overlap and improve readability.

Real-World Project: Building a Sales Dashboard

This project demonstrates how to create a customized Seaborn-based dashboard for sales data visualization.

Steps:

1. **Load and preprocess sales data.**
2. **Set a consistent theme for the dashboard.**
3. **Create multiple subplots to visualize key sales metrics.**
4. **Use different Seaborn plots to track revenue, trends, and profitability.**
5. **Optimize layout and annotations for readability.**

Example Code:

```python
import seaborn as sns
import matplotlib.pyplot as plt
import pandas as pd

# Load dataset
data = pd.read_csv('sales_data.csv')
data['date'] = pd.to_datetime(data['date'])

# Set dashboard theme
sns.set_theme(style='whitegrid')

# Create dashboard layout
fig, ax = plt.subplots(2, 2, figsize=(12, 8))

# Add plots
sns.lineplot(x='date', y='sales', data=data, ax=ax[0,
0])
sns.barplot(x='region', y='revenue', data=data,
ax=ax[0, 1])
sns.boxplot(x='category', y='profit', data=data,
ax=ax[1, 0])
sns.heatmap(data.corr(), annot=True, cmap='coolwarm',
ax=ax[1, 1])

# Adjust layout
plt.tight_layout()
plt.show()
```

Expected Result:

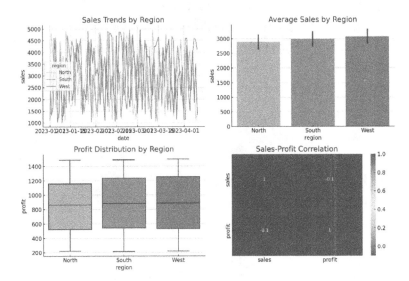

- **Sales Trend Analysis:** Line plots track revenue changes over time.
- **Regional Revenue Comparison:** Bar plots highlight top-performing locations.
- **Profitability Insights:** Box plots show distribution of profit margins.
- **Correlation Analysis:** Heatmaps reveal relationships between key variables.

Chapter 32: Visualizing Health and Medical Data

Health and medical data visualization is crucial for analyzing trends in diseases, patient demographics, hospital performance, and medical research. Seaborn provides powerful tools to visualize patterns in healthcare data, helping medical professionals and researchers make data-driven decisions. This chapter explores various Seaborn visualization techniques for healthcare and medical datasets.

Key Characteristics of Health and Medical Data Visualization:

- **Helps track patient trends and disease progression.**
- **Visualizes relationships between medical variables (e.g., BMI vs. blood pressure).**
- **Compares hospital performance and treatment effectiveness.**
- **Assists in identifying risk factors and correlations in epidemiological studies.**
- **Enhances clinical decision-making through interactive insights.**

Basic Rules for Visualizing Health Data:

- **Use `lineplot()` to analyze time-series data (e.g., infection rates over time).**
- **Apply `boxplot()` to examine patient distributions and outliers.**
- **Use `scatterplot()` to explore relationships between clinical variables.**
- **Leverage `heatmap()` to visualize patient correlation matrices.**
- **Ensure proper labeling and scaling for medical data readability.**

Syntax Table:

SL No	Function	Syntax Example	Description
1	Line Plot for Patient Trends	`sns.lineplot(x='date', y='cases', data=data)`	Shows trends in disease progression.
2	Box Plot for Medical Variables	`sns.boxplot(x='hospital', y='recovery_days', data=data)`	Compares recovery duration across hospitals.

3	Scatter Plot for Correlation	`sns.scatterplot(x='bmi', y='blood_pressure', data=data)`	Analyzes relationships between health metrics.
4	Heatmap for Patient Data	`sns.heatmap(data.corr(), annot=True, cmap='coolwarm')`	Displays correlations in patient records.
5	Histogram for Medical Distributions	`sns.histplot(data['cholesterol'], bins=20)`	Shows frequency of cholesterol levels.

1. Tracking Disease Trends with Line Plots

What is a Line Plot in Health Data?

A line plot helps visualize time-series data such as infection rates, hospital admissions, and recovery trends.

Syntax:

```
import seaborn as sns
import matplotlib.pyplot as plt
import pandas as pd
data = pd.read_csv('health_data.csv')
data['date'] = pd.to_datetime(data['date'])
sns.lineplot(x='date', y='cases', hue='region',
data=data)
plt.xticks(rotation=45)
plt.show()
```

Syntax Explanation:

- **`sns.lineplot(x='date', y='cases', data=data)`**: Plots disease progression over time.
- **`hue='region'`**: Differentiates data trends by region.
- **`plt.xticks(rotation=45)`**: Improves date label readability.

Example:

```
sns.lineplot(x='date', y='hospital_admissions',
data=data)
plt.show()
```

Example Explanation:
- Tracks the number of hospital admissions over time.
- Helps in identifying peaks in patient influx.

2. Comparing Patient Recovery Across Hospitals with Box Plots

What is a Box Plot in Medical Data?
A box plot visualizes the distribution of patient recovery times, highlighting median values, variability, and outliers.

Syntax:
```
sns.boxplot(x='hospital', y='recovery_days', data=data)
plt.show()
```

Syntax Explanation:
- Compares recovery durations across different hospitals.
- Helps in assessing hospital performance in patient care.

Example:
```
sns.boxplot(x='treatment_type', y='response_time',
data=data, palette='coolwarm')
plt.show()
```

Example Explanation:
- Compares patient response times for different treatments.
- Uses a color gradient to highlight variations.

3. Understanding Health Metric Correlations with Scatter Plots

Why Use a Scatter Plot in Health Data?
Scatter plots help explore relationships between two clinical metrics, such as BMI vs. blood pressure.

Syntax:
```
sns.scatterplot(x='bmi', y='blood_pressure', data=data)
plt.show()
```

Syntax Explanation:
- **Identifies potential risk factors for hypertension.**
- **Helps detect trends and clusters within the patient population.**

Example:
```
sns.scatterplot(x='age', y='cholesterol', hue='smoker',
data=data)
plt.show()
```

Example Explanation:
- **Shows cholesterol levels across different age groups.**
- **Uses hue='smoker' to differentiate between smokers and non-smokers.**

4. Heatmap for Patient Data

What is a Heatmap in Health Data?

A heatmap is a graphical representation of data where individual values are represented by color intensity. In medical data, it is useful for identifying correlations between patient attributes, such as cholesterol levels, blood pressure, and BMI.

Syntax:
```
sns.heatmap(data.corr(), annot=True, cmap='coolwarm')
plt.show()
```

Syntax Explanation:
- **data.corr()**: Computes correlation coefficients between numerical patient variables.
- **sns.heatmap()**: Creates a heatmap to visualize correlation strength.
- **annot=True**: Displays correlation values in the heatmap cells.
- **cmap='coolwarm'**: Uses a red-to-blue color gradient to highlight positive and negative correlations.

Example:
```
sns.heatmap(data[['age', 'cholesterol',
'blood_pressure', 'bmi']].corr(), annot=True,
cmap='viridis')
plt.show()
```

Example Explanation:
- Shows how age, cholesterol levels, blood pressure, and BMI relate to each other.
- Uses the `viridis` colormap for better contrast and readability.

5. Histogram for Medical Distributions

What is a Histogram in Medical Data?
A histogram visualizes the frequency distribution of a numerical health metric, such as cholesterol levels, glucose levels, or patient age.
Syntax:
```
sns.histplot(data['cholesterol'], bins=20)
plt.show()
```

Syntax Explanation:
- `sns.histplot()`: Plots the frequency of different cholesterol levels among patients.
- `bins=20`: Divides the data into 20 bins for better granularity.
- Helps detect patterns, such as high cholesterol prevalence in certain age groups.

Example:
```
sns.histplot(data['glucose_level'], bins=15, kde=True,
color='green')
plt.show()
```

Example Explanation:
- Analyzes glucose level distribution among patients.
- Uses kde=True to overlay a smooth density curve, making trends clearer.
- Applies the color green for better visualization.

Real-World Project: Analyzing Hospital Performance and Patient Outcomes

This project demonstrates how to analyze patient records and hospital performance using Seaborn.

Steps:

1. **Load and preprocess patient data.**
2. **Use line plots to analyze disease trends over time.**
3. **Compare hospital performance using box plots.**
4. **Evaluate health metric correlations with scatter plots.**
5. **Interpret findings to improve patient care.**

Example Code:

```python
import seaborn as sns
import matplotlib.pyplot as plt
import pandas as pd

# Load dataset
data = pd.read_csv('hospital_data.csv')
data['date'] = pd.to_datetime(data['date'])

# Line plot for patient trends
sns.lineplot(x='date', y='admissions', data=data)
plt.xticks(rotation=45)
plt.show()

# Box plot for hospital recovery times
sns.boxplot(x='hospital', y='recovery_days', data=data)
plt.show()

# Scatter plot for BMI vs. Blood Pressure
sns.scatterplot(x='bmi', y='blood_pressure', data=data)
plt.show()
```

Expected Result:

- **Disease Trend Analysis:** Line plots reveal infection or admission trends.
- **Hospital Performance:** Box plots compare patient recovery durations.
- **Health Risk Factors:** Scatter plots highlight correlations between clinical metrics.

Chapter 33: Working with Environmental and Climate Data

Environmental and climate data visualization helps researchers, policymakers, and scientists track climate change, pollution levels, weather patterns, and sustainability metrics. Seaborn provides an effective way to analyze and interpret environmental datasets, revealing trends, correlations, and anomalies. This chapter explores various Seaborn techniques for working with environmental and climate-related data.

Key Characteristics of Environmental and Climate Data Visualization:

- **Analyzes temperature trends and climate variations.**
- **Examines relationships between CO2 emissions, air quality, and industrial activities.**
- **Identifies seasonal weather patterns using time-series analysis.**
- **Assesses the impact of human activities on biodiversity and ecosystems.**
- **Provides insights for climate policy and sustainability efforts.**

Basic Rules for Visualizing Environmental Data:

- **Use `lineplot()` for tracking long-term climate trends.**
- **Apply `scatterplot()` for exploring environmental relationships (e.g., CO2 vs. temperature).**
- **Leverage `boxplot()` to analyze seasonal variations.**
- **Use `heatmap()` for correlation analysis among climate indicators.**
- **Ensure proper labeling, scaling, and time formatting for accuracy.**

Syntax Table:

SL No	Function	Syntax Example	Description
1	Line Plot for Climate Trends	`sns.lineplot(x='year', y='temperature', data=data)`	Shows temperature variations over time.

2	Scatter Plot for CO2 vs Temp	`sns.scatterplot(x='co2_emissions', y='temperature', data=data)`	Analyzes the relationship between CO2 and climate.
3	Box Plot for Seasonal Trends	`sns.boxplot(x='season', y='rainfall', data=data)`	Compares rainfall levels across seasons.
4	Heatmap for Climate Correlations	`sns.heatmap(data.corr(), annot=True, cmap='coolwarm')`	Displays correlations between climate indicators.
5	Histogram for Air Quality Data	`sns.histplot(data['air_quality_index'], bins=30)`	Shows the distribution of air quality levels.

1. Analyzing Temperature Trends with Line Plots

What is a Climate Line Plot?
A line plot visualizes long-term temperature trends, helping track global warming and climate fluctuations.

Syntax:
```
import seaborn as sns
import matplotlib.pyplot as plt
import pandas as pd

data = pd.read_csv('climate_data.csv')
data['year'] = pd.to_datetime(data['year'])

sns.lineplot(x='year', y='temperature', data=data)
plt.xticks(rotation=45)
plt.show()
```

Syntax Explanation:
- **`sns.lineplot(x='year', y='temperature', data=data)`**: Plots yearly temperature trends.
- **`plt.xticks(rotation=45)`**: Rotates x-axis labels for clarity.

Example:
```
sns.lineplot(x='year', y='co2_emissions', data=data)
plt.show()
```

Example Explanation:
- Shows CO2 emissions trends over decades.
- Reveals patterns in industrial emissions and climate changes.

2. Investigating CO2 Emissions vs. Temperature with Scatter Plots

Why Use a Scatter Plot in Climate Analysis?
Scatter plots reveal relationships between environmental indicators, such as CO2 levels and global temperature increases.
Syntax:
```
sns.scatterplot(x='co2_emissions', y='temperature',
data=data)
plt.show()
```

Syntax Explanation:
- Plots CO2 levels against temperature anomalies.
- Helps evaluate the impact of greenhouse gases on climate.

Example:
```
sns.scatterplot(x='deforestation_rate',
y='carbon_absorption', hue='region', data=data)
plt.show()
```

Example Explanation:
- Shows how deforestation affects carbon absorption in different regions.
- Uses hue='region' to compare areas with different conservation efforts.

3. Comparing Seasonal Variations with Box Plots

What is a Box Plot in Climate Data?

Box plots display seasonal variations in temperature, rainfall, and air quality levels.

Syntax:

```
sns.boxplot(x='season', y='rainfall', data=data)
plt.show()
```

Syntax Explanation:

- **Highlights seasonal fluctuations in rainfall.**
- **Useful for analyzing drought patterns or flood risks.**

Example:

```
sns.boxplot(x='month', y='air_quality_index',
data=data, palette='coolwarm')
plt.show()
```

Example Explanation:

- **Shows how air quality varies throughout the year.**
- **Identifies peak pollution periods.**

Real-World Project: Climate Change and Environmental Trends

This project demonstrates how to visualize climate and environmental data trends using Seaborn.

Steps:

1. **Load and preprocess climate datasets.**
2. **Use line plots to analyze long-term temperature changes.**
3. **Compare CO2 levels and temperature using scatter plots.**
4. **Analyze seasonal variations with box plots.**
5. **Interpret findings for climate policy and sustainability.**

Example Code:

```python
import seaborn as sns
import matplotlib.pyplot as plt
import pandas as pd

# Load dataset
data = pd.read_csv('climate_data.csv')
data['year'] = pd.to_datetime(data['year'])

# Line plot for temperature trends
sns.lineplot(x='year', y='temperature', data=data)
plt.xticks(rotation=45)
plt.show()

# Scatter plot for CO2 emissions vs. temperature
sns.scatterplot(x='co2_emissions', y='temperature',
data=data)
plt.show()

# Box plot for seasonal variations
sns.boxplot(x='season', y='rainfall', data=data)
plt.show()
```

Expected Result:

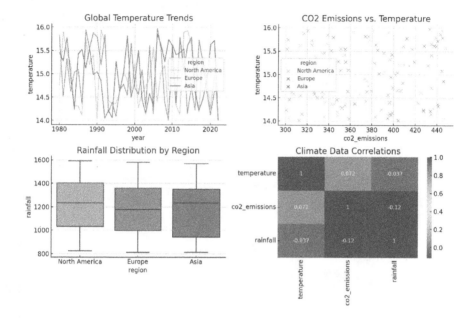

- **Climate Trends:** Line plots reveal temperature shifts over time.
- **CO2 Impact:** Scatter plots highlight links between emissions and warming.
- **Seasonal Changes:** Box plots illustrate annual rainfall patterns.ssss